GRIE[F]
is
NOT
my
FUTURE

Because I have

a Glorious Eternal Purpose

Marla Aycock

You're Never Alone!

Matt 1:23

Marla Aycock

CONTENTS

Chapter 1

Things Are Not What They Seem

August 2010

Only one distant thunderhead hinted of a storm.

August, notorious for sultry weather, rarely veered from its course. But the previous cool night created a light breeze. The weight of daily responsibilities morphed into light-hearted energy as I drove the winding backroads toward my daughter's home.

My sister, Katrina, had reserved a condo for a week at a mountain resort in North Georgia. Esther my twenty-six-year-old daughter, tagged along for just the weekend, so we met at her home and caravanned our cars north.

Katrina gifted us with the master suite of the condo, so Esther and I would be roomies. Esther, my kindred spirit, reflected my joy at having this extended time together.

First to arrive, we strolled the resort property. The fresh country air and wide-open spaces expanded our spirits as our eyes absorbed the life-giving green of hills and fields. Gravel crunched as Katrina wheeled into the parking lot a short time later. We checked in, delighted to find we were in a new V.I.P. unit. I smiled and thought, *definitely a God-hug.*

Our playful laughter filled the air as we exited the resort office and I reached over and plucked three stems of wild grass for each to chew in rural hayseed-style. Retrieving our luggage and adding a bit of sashay to our walk, we entered the condo, a perfect blend of Country-Chic. Later, Esther and I giggled like teenagers as we unpacked in our elegant room.

◎◎◎

Early the next morning, the rising sun glistened through billows of fog and enticed me outside for a walk. When I returned a muffled groan stopped me in mid-stride before I entered the condo. Looking for the source, I leaned over the wrought-iron railing listening intently. Once again, the disturbing sound. I questioned—*Is it an animal? A person?* The air went quiet. I waited, but only birdsong and the humming of bees lingered. The sun rose full, chasing away any remnant of shadows.

I decided to make coffee for the sleepyheads still tucked away in slumber-land.

While pouring my first cup, I heard the whimpering moans again. I followed the sound, surprised to find they led to our closed bedroom door. Silently, I entered and viewed Esther's crumpled form across the bed. Unaware of my presence, her cries turned into sweet humming as lyrics and melody of Chris Tomlin's worship song followed...*I will rise, when He calls my name...no more sorrow, no more pain...I will rise on eagle's wings... before my God fall on my knees.*

My heart seized tight like a fist clenching a precious jewel, and my mother-antennae sprang to full alert. Rushing to her, I said, "Esther, honey, how could you be in so much pain and not tell me? Have you seen a doctor?"

Hesitating, she answered. "No, Marmie, remember I don't have medical insurance. I keep missing the window of time to sign-up." She breathed a great sigh, expressing frustration at her ineptness and covered her face with both hands.

"I remember, but the important thing right now is for you to receive the care you need."

She had complained off and on for several months but her past excellent health never gave me reason for concern. However, in this more intimate space I noticed how loose her clothes hung. A biting fear pierced my heart as I stared with new awareness at her gaunt form. Suddenly, my instincts knew her pain could *not* be a minor issue.

I said goodbye to her late Sunday afternoon with a playful sternness and instructions: "Tomorrow you call a doctor and get in to see him immediately. I will check with you in the morning to make sure you follow through. If you don't, I'm coming to your house, tie you up, throw you in the car and take you myself!" We chuckled at my unusual terseness, but she knew I meant it.

Esther, in too much pain to go to work on Monday, necessitated my trip to her home. Tension crackled as her husband searched online for a doctor. He mentioned how intense Esther's pain had been at times—even to the point of screaming out in agony. My fierce anger butted hard against churning dread. Silently, I raged. *Why didn't you take steps to get her help?* With an appointment set for Wednesday, I took her back to the resort with me.

Esther would rather suffer in silence than cause inconvenience or worry to others, so her involuntary scream when the doctor examined her on Wednesday confirmed my fears.

The doctor explained, "I can feel a mass in her lower colon. She needs to see a surgeon."

Bluntly, I asked, "Do you think it's cancer?"

He answered, "I'm ninety-percent sure it's not."

Comforted by those odds, a measure of peace soothed our jangled nerves as we returned to the resort.

We had scheduled Esther's appointment with the recommended surgeon for the following week, but by Friday morning her pain had intensified. Back at home, my husband, Seth, contacted the surgeon's office and pleaded with the staff to fit her in immediately. Even though they were booked solid with appointments and surgeries all day, my bull-dog husband achieved what seemed impossible. By that afternoon, Seth spoke directly with the doctor and convinced him to stay late and perform the exploratory out-patient-surgery.

Frenzied packing followed as Esther and I had an hour-and-a-half to make a two-hour trip.

☺☺☺

Esther, swept away to be prepped for surgery, left me in an office cubicle handing the hospital clerk a significant deposit. Seth arrived and we were directed to a large open waiting area. We sat side by side with tense postures as fear snaked along taut nerves.

A lady dressed in green hospital scrubs sat in a row of chairs facing us. Seth, never one to meet a stranger, struck up a conversation which brought some much-needed diversion. She seemed to be on break or maybe waiting for a ride home.

My mind whirled with thoughts of Esther when I remembered pain meds could be hard to obtain after-hours on weekends. Our pharmacy would be closed by the time we arrived home so I nudged Seth and asked him to see if the woman could give us directions to one in the area.

"I'm sorry, I can't help you as I'm not from around here," she replied.

Seth made a successful inquiry at the information desk and quickly left to get Esther's pain meds.

A kind concern etched the face of the lady in scrubs as I shared our deep concern for Esther. She leaned forward. Her dark shoulder-length hair framed her olive complexion as she expressed encouragement with a compassionate gentle voice:

"I have a special feeling about your family. You will get through this."

We chatted until the call came—Esther had entered the recovery room.

Stunned, I realized Esther's husband had not arrived. My call found him still working at home. My words were etched with an angry impatience. I urged, "Please hurry, I know the doctor will want to speak with you."

A short time later the surgeon requested a meeting with family members. Esther's husband hadn't arrived and Seth had not returned from the pharmacy. Alone, with a wooden-legged gait and nails pressed hard into palms, I entered the small sterile consult room. The surgeon bore an unreadable countenance. With little preface, he raised his sizable clenched hand and said, "I'm sorry to tell you, but I removed a cancerous tumor from your daughter larger than my fist."

The blunt news stunned and flattened me. I'd clung to the first doctor's assessment. I hadn't expected her to be in the small 10 % of possibilities.

Shell shocked, I massaged my temples in an effort to clear the fog. I needed to think of an intelligent question, but my thoughts scattered like pellets from a shotgun. On the edge of a major meltdown, an army of desperate questions barraged my mind:

Where is Esther's husband?

Where is Seth? He's so good at thinking on his feet in a crisis!

Why do I have to hear this alone?

I saw the doctor's lips move, but could not comprehend his foreign words. Commanding myself to focus, I realized he was explaining her type of cancer. My trembling fingers searched my purse for pen and paper. I requested the doctor write out the strange words, *squamous cell cancer.* Beyond that, the details blurred. Only the clattering phrase, "Your daughter has cancer," resonated.

As I left the consult room, a strange numbness settled into my feet and legs, making it difficult to navigate. I reached for a chair to stabilize me as I entered an alternate reality; another world where I could see what was happening around me, but felt detached.

Zombie-like, I returned to the waiting area as vibrations of shock seemed to ooze from every pore. Some people explode in emotion at such news; I tend to implode with an internal meltdown and go numb.

Esther's husband arrived. His questioning dark eyes met mine, as I simply said, "She has cancer." He turned abruptly and walked out of the hospital without saying a word. I assumed he needed time to process the news.

Through tears difficult to control, I shared the grim news with Seth when he returned from the pharmacy. We held each other and wept.

While we waited to be called to the recovery room, I stepped into a quiet alcove to contact family members and church friends. I believe in the power of prayer and I knew we desperately needed support. Esther and our family were put on numerous prayer chains across the country.

I first called Esther's older sister, Jayne. Her voice broke with the shock of the news as she blurted, "No! I should be the one not *her*. She doesn't deserve this!"

I, the Momma—protector of my children's hearts—still tear up at the memory of her response. In part, my dearly loved first-born would eventually find her way to inner healing and wholeness because of the valley we were about to walk. In truth, our family and close friends would all have our faith tested.

Returning to the waiting area, my eyes traced the wet spider patterns on Seth's cheeks. Once again, our lady-in-green engaged him in conversation. He seemed to have aged years instead of hours since we arrived. I sat and snuggled my hand in his as she told us a moving story of a friend who survived cancer and went on to live a productive life. Inspired, our spirits lifted.

Jolted back to the present, my hand vibrated as the pager buzzed. Like a sudden arctic blast, my thoughts froze as I realized time had come to tell my daughter the ugly life-altering news. In the recovery room, and more alert than I expected, Esther peppered me with questions. I chose to ease into the results of the surgery and dodged most of her queries. Finally, I said, "Let's just focus on getting you home and settled." We gathered her belongings and instructions for her post-surgery care.

As a nurse rolled Esther's wheelchair to our car, our cheerleader in hospital greens joined us and affirmed her with reassuring words. After I gently eased Esther into the backseat with pillows and blankets, I turned to say a final good-bye to our new encouraging friend. With her warm hug and gentle kiss on my cheek I settled into the front seat. Her enthusiastic wave sent us on our way.

On the drive home, my thoughts tumbled atop each other...

This cannot be.

She's so healthy.

She's rarely sick.

She's always taken good care of herself.

Our family has never experienced cancer.

As her friends and family heard the news, similar comments were made.

"Impossible! No way! If Esther can get cancer, anyone can get cancer!"

Later, I learned squamous cell is a slow growing external cancer. Esther's, internal and rare, resulted in a more complex situation.

Esther requested I be her caregiver as her husband's work didn't allow him to be as available. I settled her into our downstairs master bedroom and eased myself down beside her. Puzzled over the lady in green scrubs. I commented, "Esther, this kind lady at the hospital..." With a deft movement her hand clasped my forearm and stopped me mid-sentence, "Marmie, she was an angel." There was a glow to her face and a sureness in her voice like iron. Although startled by her words, I couldn't dismiss her response. She had a heart sensitive to spiritual things.

I stopped and reflected—wondering—could she be right?

She appeared to be medical personnel on break, *but* she lingered with us for several hours. When we asked for directions, she'd said, "I'm not from around here." She had no purse, cell phone, car keys or personal belongings. She'd sat there, a perfect stranger, quietly interjecting the encouragement we so needed.

As an earth dweller, I may never know for sure, but —was she?

Psalms 91:11 NIV
For he will command his angels concerning you to guard you in all your ways.

REFLECT

How or where in your life have you seen God show up during a time of trial or grief? Have you ever experienced what you thought might be a heavenly messenger? How did the experience effect or change you?

APPLY

Do you realize, whatever crisis you're experiencing or diagnosis you've received might be *some* of the truth, but it's not *all* the truth? Have you written your God-moment down? If so, pull out your journal and read it. If not, write it out now. Look for new insights and encouragement to apply to your present situation. Read Psalm 73 aloud. Print it out and keep it close.

PRAYER

Heavenly Father, in Psalms 34:18 you said you're close to me, the brokenhearted, and you rescue me when my spirit is crushed. Grief has entered my world in a way I never expected and I feel like I'm bleeding out and you're not there. So, by faith I speak truth into the dark; your Word is truth. Psalm 31:7 says I'm to be glad and rejoice in your unfailing love, for you see my trouble and You *care* about the anguish of my soul.

Chapter 2

People Are Not Who They Seem

Marmie Meets Romeo

December 2005

The stranger slid up to our small table as if he had a right to be there.

As Esther and I waited to be seated at the restaurant, I'd noticed him across the room as he raked his eyes over an unassuming young woman. I recognized the type. I didn't want him near my daughter. When I realized he intended to interrupt my time with Esther, I wanted to yank the chair from under him.

Between my work and Esther's studies there had been little *we* time. *Our* special moment—Christmas shopping with a late lunch and time to catch up on life, did not include a male intrusion.

Located close to the university, Esther explained she and a girlfriend often came to this restaurant midafternoon for a salad and to study. Then I understood; she'd met him before.

He joined us. Soft-spoken with a foreign accent, I strained to hear him. His cupped hand partially covering his mouth added to my annoyance. I kept expecting him to leave. He didn't. His mannerisms reminded me of practiced deception as one would see from an undercover agent. Later, disappointed and fatigued by the encounter, I stepped outside with Esther. The damp chill in the air reflected my opinion as I looked at her and said, "You realize he's a spy, right?"

Unaware—I'd just met Esther's Romeo.

A mysterious man with a past who wanted my daughter in his future.

ⓔⓔⓔ

The previous June a grand celebration had commenced — Esther's twenty-first birthday.

Esther loved to investigate new flavors of tea, so she and I had made a hobby of exploring nearby tea rooms and sampling all their delicacies. From scones and clotted cream to the tangy delight of lemon curd—our tongues tingled at the thought.

So, for her special day, I had planned a high tea for her at a friend's spacious home complete with caterers and a special guest speaker to present a history of tea. Her girlfriends arrived and we provided ladies old-fashioned hats and other accessories to add vintage elegance to their attire. Little did she know she would meet a mysterious tea connoisseur that very evening who would set the wheels of her future in motion.

After the tea, Esther and several friends rendezvoused at a favorite restaurant. What an unlikely place to meet her Romeo who seemed to share her fascination with tea—an aficionado of sorts. Dark, handsome and mysterious, he didn't allow the twelve-year age difference to hinder his pursuit of her, nor she, her fascination with him.

Esther's Perspective

In Esther's opinion, the stars seemed to align when Romeo entered her life. She connected with him on many levels. Their mutual love of art, history, music, and world travel created a special bond and both were avid readers. His physical prowess and martial art skills made her feel safe and protected. It seemed to her he'd be a faithful companion who would provide stimulating conversation as well.

His incredible story of arriving in the United States because of his involvement with a group of Korean Christian missionaries had Esther wide-eyed and wonder-struck. To her, a man with such an impressive background who had been involved with a Christian ministry, seemed a logical possibility for a long-term relationship.

Not long before this, Esther's heart had been wounded by the betrayal of a young man we thought would become a part of our family. This created a soft target for the arrow launched when Romeo suggested he and Esther make a *pact of loyalty* when they started dating a short time later. To me, her previous relationship with a man who proved unfaithful and a failed marriage in Romeo's past, explained their need for this.

His childhood stories of a harsh life captured Esther's tender heart, but actions he considered normal, some would qualify as cruel. Besides an angry abusive father, one story stands out. As a young boy, an intoxicated dentist broke a needle off in his gum. When Romeo screamed in pain the dentist slapped him so hard he saw stars. The dentist bellowed shame at his sissy response with, "take it like a man!" As our relationship unfolded over time, I saw an unbalanced mind-set had formed. *Pain is good because it just makes you stronger.* A definite concern.

Esther's two-week trip to the Ukraine as a teenager further strengthened their connection, as this linked her to a circle of friends in the Atlanta area who shared Romeo's background. Fascinated by other cultures, she naturally became captivated by Romeo's colorful past.

Romeo's personal history was complicated but intriguing to Esther. However, to more mature ears, troubling.

We, her family, were not *formally* introduced to Romeo as a person of interest until eight months later in February of 2006. In hindsight, there had been too much hiding and secrecy.

Not fitting into our family dynamics or beliefs well, much contention arrived with him. A failed marriage, foreign atheistic background, and their age difference were valid reasons for our family's concern.

☉☉☉

Stories Romeo shared with Me

Over the two years they dated I worked hard at establishing a good relationship with Romeo. I read a 1,000-page book about his country's history and watched related movies with him. I listened to his views on religion and politics.

A parent walks a fine line when their child starts dating. Rejecting the object of their affection causes them to go into a defense mode and bring a rift in the parent-child relationship. Since meeting him at the restaurant, my Momma-heart felt unsettled. Esther knew of my concern and skepticism of this stranger and tried hard to convince me of his amazing qualities.

"Please Marmie, give him a chance and get to know him, his story is remarkable!"

Romeo often spent evenings at our home telling me his life stories as Esther studied or retired early due to morning classes.

I had many questions, and this time provided a chance to ask them: "So, tell me about your years in the military? Were you ever in danger? What was your training like? Did you ever face combat? After being so intent on being a soldier, what was the tipping point which caused you to opt out?"

His answers were more puzzling than informative, but the key seemed to be a talk he'd had with his military father plus reading some private writings of Vladimir Lenin he'd gained access to.

This, along with Romeo's innuendo, vague explanations and my own unfamiliarity with his culture kept me off balance and confused. James Bond movies and missionary reports about his country's persecution of Christians didn't help.

One night while discussing his past military experiences in his usual surreptitious manner, he told me a spine-tingling story. "As I returned from a military mission and boarded a train. I sat across from two rough-looking soldiers. They seemed edgy, like time bombs only needing a spark to set them off. They hurled drunken taunts at me and I ignored them as best I could. They seemed to be asking for a fight. Out-numbered plus their burly stature kept me quiet until they made derogatory comments about my mother. They'd crossed an unacceptable line and I lost it."

I leaned forward. "So, what happened?"

"I only have a vague memory of the aftermath. I remember walking away from the train a bit dazed, and when I looked back, the windows of the car I'd been in were covered with red smears."

I assumed from the context of the story they had to be blood, but it was late and I don't think I really wanted to know. Sometimes, after such an evening, I'd be so troubled I would go to my room and pound the wall with my fists before climbing into bed and ask God, "Why? Why him?" Fear and turmoil plagued my spirit.

Romeo's father, his hero, served in the military in the country's chief government agency of internal security, intelligence and secret police. As a young boy, Romeo dreamed of following in his father's footsteps and becoming a soldier too. Even when Romeo's athletic skills opened an opportunity to train for the Olympics, he chose the military. Early each morning, his father woke him to a routine of weight lifting and fitness training.

☺☺☺

At seven years of age the military relocated Romeo's family to Poland where he spent the next seven years and learned Polish. By the time he finished his school years, he'd become fluent in several languages.

According to Romeo, his lifelong desire to be a soldier became reality when he graduated with honors from the top military school of his homeland. There, Romeo became fluent in Korean to fulfill his role as an intelligence agent. Assigned to a border post, he gathered information to assist his country. But during a political upheaval which restructured his country's boundaries and government in the 1980's, Romeo lost his passion for soldiering and left the military.

New employment emerged when a prominent Asian figure visited Romeo's country on business and hired him as his translator. This opened another opportunity to translate for a mission group of young people visiting his country. Ironically, Romeo, raised in an atheistic culture, traveled with them translating the Gospel of Jesus Christ.

When the group traveled to the United States, Romeo, fluent in English, came with them. When the Asian group moved on to another country, Romeo (without proper documents) stayed behind and traveled the U.S. with the group's leader. They visited major cities along the West Coast, then headed east across America, ending in New York City.

After some menial employment, he studied to take a securities exam and became an investment broker, which eventually led him to Atlanta. Experiencing success in his new job, he branched out and began his own business with two other men. This ended in devastating betrayal by his partners, resulting in a year of crippling depression.

His mother, Zia, arrived in the U.S. and helped him get back on his feet. He soon became assistant manager of the restaurant where he first met Esther on her twenty-first birthday.

Red Flags

Consistently throughout the two years of their dating and engagement, Esther's Father, Seth, voiced strong objections to her relationship with Romeo, stating: "He's not who you think he is!" Her sister, Jayne, also had strong negative reactions.

Generally, our family didn't watch R-rated movies and the ones Romeo brought were violent. They crossed a line for our family, so we requested he not bring them. Later, he rented his all-time favorite movie, "Nicholas and

Alexandra." A winner of several Academy Awards in 1971, the photography, acting, and historical accounts were well done.

Three hours later, as I rewound the videotape, Romeo's statement caused my heart to shudder. He praised the self-absorbed, weak, and insensitive leadership of Czar Nicholas and stated the relationship between Nicholas and Alexandra to be the greatest love story of all time.

I guffawed aloud. With some background in psychology and my personal emotional healing, I knew Nicolas and Alexandria's marriage reeked of psychological dysfunction. His view of what made a good leader and a healthy relationship haunted me. When I spoke to Esther of my concern, she agreed, but seemed blinded to the depth of its implications.

But my Momma-heart knew from the beginning he was *not* a good match for her. Marriage in itself is a huge challenge: add an agnostic background, a foreign culture, opposite political views, a prior divorce, and a twelve-year age difference and the odds of the marriage succeeding are slim.

But—my daughter seemed to love this man.

Clearly, I needed a different perspective, her perspective. So, I went to one of the most treasured gifts Esther left me—her journals. I read. I cried. I prayed.

Then I began to see Romeo through Esther's eyes. My spiritual gift of mercy softened my heart toward him. I don't believe anyone is beyond redemption.

I found it helpful as I walked through the corridors of her life in her own handwriting and read about her love for him. As I saw Romeo through my daughter's lens, I could let go of some of the anger and also acknowledge his redeeming qualities.

I remembered how he exhibited a kind tenderness toward children and animals—especially dogs. Both he and his mother were not only kind to my special needs' daughter, they seemed drawn to her. I saw silent tears slide down Romeo's cheek when he listened to children's performances at church. It helped me remember why Esther had fallen in love with him. And she certainly had. After an eight-month engagement, she married him.

However, Esther's sweetness and patience worked against her as the marriage deteriorated within the first year. It's so hard to see through the fog of one's first romantic assessments and realize a purposed manipulation could be taking place.

Esther's written prayers in her journal exhibited a raw vulnerability and courage as she faced not only her cancer but the contention within her marriage.

Consistently, she surrendered to her Heavenly Father in the midst of it all.

For me, from the time I first met Romeo, an unsettling complexity knotted my stomach and kept me feeling uneasy and confused. For me, something seemed broken in him—maybe even unsafe.

REFLECT

Have you ever made a life-altering choice in the rift of a broken heart? Is your present pain the result of that unwise decision? Are you grasping at straws to stay afloat?

APPLY

Even the wisest of us get deceived or misdirected, sometimes even if we've sought counsel. But *time* is needed for our heart to heal when it's broken.

If you're in a relationship that's questionable and friends or family are giving you push-back. If your parent is warning you, *this person is not who you think they are*, be wise and listen. Men read other men better in most circumstances, so listen to your father. The same with sons—mom's read other women more accurately. Give proper weight to their counsel. Our parents and friends want to save us from future heartache and regret. Love *is* often blind.

Memorize Proverbs 4:23 NLT

Guard your heart above all else,

for it determines the course of your life.

Read the book, "Cherish," by Gary Thomas which gives good insight and counsel.

PRAYER

Dear Heavenly Father, I know your plans for me are good. Help me to listen to wisdom from your Word and those who love and care about me. Establish in me a healthy heart.

Chapter 3

Disordered Loves

God is all about people having healthy relationships. Esther was an oasis in the deserts of my life. Someone to mutually enjoy God's gifts of creation. Awe of His artistry in everything from a stunning sunrise to an unusual shell on a beach thrilled and inspired us. Our love of music and fun piano duets caused our hearts to beat in sync. Our mutual faith allowed us a special fellowship. Both "foodies" we enjoyed trying new dishes. Sushi. Lasagna or high tea. Unique desserts with a fresh cup of coffee put us over the moon. The list is extensive and wonderful.

Then, an early morning intrusion jabbed my heart.

The convicting words poked and prodded, nudging me from an exhausted sleep.

You shall have no other gods before me,

You shall have no other gods before me,

You shall have no other gods before me.

Startled, my eyes opened wide. I thought, *could it be true—Esther had become a god to me?*

I realized how desperate I was to hang on to her and how adrift and hollow I felt at just the thought of losing her. She was a delight and encouragement to me on so many levels; without Esther I didn't want to live. The emotional trauma of her surgery and diagnosis of cancer had turned my world into a frightening shadowed landscape.

The thought Esther had become an idol shocked me, yet the conviction was clear and specific. I knew the path to peace as I stumbled out of bed and sprawled facedown. By an act of *faith,* the Lord was directing me to surrender Esther to Him. I was to trust Him no matter what.

As I lay on the proverbial wrestling mat with God, I thought of Abraham when God asked him to sacrifice Isaac on an altar—his long-awaited miracle-son. I think like me, Abraham's love for his child was beautiful, but had become disordered. *God knows how tenuous our faith is if its foundation is built around something or someone that can be taken away.*

Abraham and his wife Sarah lived in a culture where a woman's worth was tied directly to an ability to produce children, especially an heir. I thought about the long wait, frustrations, and snide remarks of prideful friends and family during the many years of Sarah's barrenness. The rolling eyes of silent judgements by relatives and comrades of Abraham as he claimed God had promised he would be the father of many nations with descendants too numerous to count.

Then, the miraculous conception and unbridled jubilation of Isaacs birth. Wrinkled hands caressing fresh silken baby skin and crinkly lips against plump cheeks. The joy, the wonder, the miracle of it all. These facts alone would wrap a parent's heart into the widest love-knot imaginable.

His very name meant *laughter*. Is there anything sweeter and more delightful than a baby's giggles? Can you imagine the household of Abraham? The atmosphere infused with the rapturous mirth would have affected servants from highest to lowest rank. Sarah's role as a mother realized. Abraham's heir from his own loins— God's promise fulfilled. Abraham and Sarah's relationship with Isaac overflowed with the purest joy. God delights in such relationships.

So why, in all that's called sacred, would God ask Abraham to sacrifice this precious child of promise?

Because maybe unknown to Abraham, his love for Isaac had become greater than his love for God. *Thou shalt have no other gods before me,* had to be tested. Not for God's knowledge as He's omniscient, but for the strengthening and refining of Abraham's faith. He still had seventy-five more years of life and ministry to fulfill.

Although Genesis 22 doesn't reveal anything regarding a resistance by Abraham to God's instructions to sacrifice his beloved son on an altar, the thought of plunging a knife into him had to have shaken him to his core. I believe it may have been a long sleepless night of immeasurable struggle. Maybe it's why in verse three he's up *early* loading his donkey.

Genesis 22:1-2 and 12b NLT

Sometime later, God tested Abraham's faith.

"Abraham!" God called.

"Yes," he replied. "Here I am."

'Take your son, your only son—yes, Isaac, whom you love so much—and go to the land of Moriah.

Go and sacrifice him as a burnt offering on one of the
mountains, which I will show you.

God interrupts Abraham…

Do not hurt him in any way,
for now I know that you truly fear God.
You have not withheld from me even your son…

☉☉☉

I fixated on a smudged carpet fiber as I laid on the floor humbled, and remembered I'd been at the crossroads of yielding before—times when the choice to trust the Lord seemed impossible—even crazy.

Moments of surrender in my past dealt with facing the trauma of childhood abuse, the life-long challenge of raising a special needs' child, which in turn influenced another daughter's unhealthy life choices.

But this? The possible *death* of a beloved daughter? To yield to the horror of that?!

My mother heart remained tethered to my child. I could *not* release her.

After a great struggle the floodgates opened and through curtains of liquid surrender, I sobbed, "Lord, I choose to trust you by an act of my *will*, but You will have to do the soul surgery, I can't let go!"

From a deep place, an emotional purge began as God's Spirit led me to the foot of the cross where my Father God had allowed His *perfect* Holy Son to be sacrificed for *me*. My constricted heart calmed as my grasping hands opened.

Astonished, I realized by placing her in the loving arms of her Savior, Jesus, the *true* sacrificial lamb; live or die, she was safe. He'd already defeated death through his resurrection.

Much later while reading through Esther's journal, she revealed how God worked through this time to prepare her for the trial ahead. In His omniscience He led us both to realign the order of our love with Him as our primary passion.

Jesus, our Emmanuel, the lover of our soul!

REFLECT

Is faith something you can manufacture without the trial? Can gold become pure without the fire? Can you win a battle without the warfare? Can new life sprout without the seed first dying?

APPLY

As counter-intuitive as it sounds, please embrace the process you're in. I'm not suggesting a naïve idealistic approach. Get on the wrestling mat with God and pour out all your honest angry questions and accusations. God wants you hot or cold, and real. He can handle it.

Please know, your present trial is an opportunity for your faith to soar like an eagle; for the fiery trial to refine and purify you, revealing eternal treasures worth more than gold; the war allows practice and new strength in wielding your spiritual armor (Ephesians 6:10-18) which leads to victory and peace, and what seems dead will emerge into new life.

PRAYER

Heavenly Father, I choose to embrace my present trial, knowing as I surrender to you, giving proper order to the things I love, you will use it for your glory and my good.

Romans 8:28. KJV

*And we know that all things work together for good to
them that love God,
to them who are called according to his purpose.*

Thank you for the saints who've walked before me and demonstrated your love. I know you'll do the same for me. You will not leave me in the dark to wander alone.

Chapter 4

Vision and a Wall of Warriors

Ephesians 6:12 NIV

For our struggle is not against flesh and blood,

but against the rulers, against the authorities,

against the powers of this dark world

and against the spiritual forces of evil in the heavenly

realms.

Early one morning, shortly after Esther's surgery, I entered a twilight consciousness from an exhausted sleep. I heard loud buzzing as a large screen lowered before me. It displayed a crystal-clear picture as I became both audience and participant along with Seth, and Esther. We stood atop a hill overlooking a rolling green terrain. A winding road snaked through it. We experienced a sweet camaraderie just being together. No audible conversation was exchanged among the three of us, just an internal understanding. The landscape seemed peaceful yet contained an uneasiness due to the complete silence and absence of movement.

We heard the low hum of a motor, and from our right an old-fashioned prop plane flew across the highway in front of us. It seemed the pilot was out for a leisurely ride as it slowly disappeared over the horizon. The event seemed passive but the atmosphere carried an unsettling eeriness. Soon the sound of louder engines revealed two more similar aircraft from the left which moved slowly off to our right. (I discovered later, in times of war, this is called a reconnaissance mission to obtain information by visual observation of an enemy.)

In the distant sky we began to see small dots appear —perhaps a large flock of birds? Next, we heard a low-pitched rumbling as vibrations tingled the soles of our feet. Then a deafening roar rolled over us as the heavens filled with indiscriminate dark objects. The uneasiness quickly became alarm. The dark specks pressed closer and we observed an army of planes as far as the eye could see. Strangely, they appeared to be from a WW I movie; exposed pilots flew propeller-driven aircraft with open cockpits. As the first one flew over our heads, an evil looking creature leaned over the side and with a calculated leering gleam, pointed directly at us. There were no words spoken, but it was clear we were in his crosshairs and he intended to destroy us. Then the screen went black and disappeared.

Stunned and a bit freaked out, I woke fully and shared the dream with Esther. She said, "Marmie, what you saw fits perfect with my life verses on spiritual warfare in Ephesians 6." One thing became clear to me— we as a family were entering a time of great spiritual battle.

Later, I thought, *did I have a vision?* I'm not sure what I believed before, but I know hearing about a vision and experiencing one are worlds apart, even mind bending. I'd never had anything happen like that before, yet in the book of Joel, he writes:

And it shall come to pass afterward that I will pour out
my Spirit on all flesh;
Your sons' and your daughters shall prophesy,
Your old men shall dream dreams,
Your young men shall see visions.

Distraught, I asked repeatedly throughout the next few days, "God, why would you let me see that? What possible good could it serve when I'm already so traumatized?"

During the days of post-operative care at our home, there had been great tension and disagreements among family members. Esther was adamant she would try alternative treatments *first*. Her husband and her dad, Seth, agreed chemo and radiation *should* be her choice.

Contention, fear, and confusion swirled around us like a sandstorm mixed with thorns as Esther left our house to return home. *Contention*, because of great disagreement within the family, *fear*, because we knew this was a life and death situation, *confusion*, as we understood so little about her cancer.

A week later found me pacing the living room and replaying the vision over and over in my mind. Repeatedly, with a deliberate foot stomp for emphasis, I shouted, "God, Why? Why did you let me see that?"

An internal command halted my angry barrage. "Turn around!" The words were so explicit and compelling I *physically* turned around. Simultaneously, my *mind's eye* saw a great wall reaching from earth to heaven with what appeared to be the throne of God at the pinnacle. Cascading from it were heavenly beings— golden and glistening with an unearthly light. Some were on horses and others stood with swords drawn ready for battle. Mentally, I revisited my previous frightening scene. The planes had shrunk to the size of black gnats. Powerless. Harmless. The lies and death threat of the enemy were exposed. Peace fell and fear fled.

Why did God let me see that? John 16:33 revealed His answer.

"I have told you these things,

so that in me you may have peace.

In this world you will have trouble.

But take heart! I have overcome the world."

More confirmation came as the story of the prophet Elisha came to mind.

2 Kings 6:15-17

"When the servant of the man of God got up and went out early the next morning, an army

with horses and chariots had surrounded the city.

"Oh no, my lord! What shall we do?" the servant asked.

"Don't be afraid," the prophet answered.

"Those who are with us are more than those who are with them."

And Elisha prayed, "Open his eyes, LORD, so that he may see."

Then the LORD opened the servant's eyes, and he looked and saw the hills full of horses and chariots of fire all around Elisha.

Like Elisha, the Lord allowed me a glimpse into the heavenly realms and then revealed the powerlessness of my enemy. I knew from that point on the spiritual battle would be fierce, but as the lady in green scrubs had said, *we would make it through this.*

The vision of the wall of warriors comforted me in this present battle and would bring encouragement with new significance in the future. The Lord wastes nothing.

Of one thing I am perfectly sure; God's story never ends with ashes.

Elisabeth Elliot

REFLECT

We shouldn't be afraid of visions from God as he promises they will be a real part of the end times before He returns. Why does God give visions? He's either shedding light on an attack coming from your enemy or for something He, God himself is about to do. This may happen more in the end times as there will be so much misinformation. How do we know if a vision is from God? Satan never gives us a vision of hope, sacrificial giving, or of evil being defeated.

APPLY

The majority of people I know do not have visions, but God's Word in Joel is very clear: they're real. The litmus test to know if they're from God is, they line up with His Word and what's been foretold, happens. Above all, do *not* start chasing visions, dreams, or the supernatural. Stay focused on *Jesus*. Our enemy, the devil, (and yes, he's real), is a deceiver who loves to distract and confuse us so we'll take our eyes off of Jesus, the true source of our power.

PRAYER

Dear Heavenly Father,

As mesmerizing as the supernatural is, may I always keep my eyes on your Son, Jesus, who is the Way, the Truth, and the Life. Give me wisdom and sensitivity to the red flags signaling danger and deception from the enemy. Your Word states in Proverbs 4:23 to guard my heart above all else because it will determine the course of my life. Father, my eyes are on you.

Chapter 5

The Matrix of Medical Choices

It is better to take refuge in the LORD

than to trust in man.

Psalm 118:8 NIV

As a mom, the matrix of life and death choices regarding cancer treatments were overwhelming: *Cut* via surgery, *poison* with chemotherapy, *burn* by radiation and *dependence on drugs*. Those were the primary choices of conventional cures for cancer. It takes a lot of personal research, conviction, and tenacity to buck the system and choose another route. It's not for everyone. (There's no guarantee regardless of what you choose).

Ever since Esther's cancer diagnoses, the underlying current of contention which permeated our family concerning treatment became an added pressure for her, but this choice did not come without extensive research and thought.

As a child, my family had the best medical insurance available, and we chose only conventional methods of health care. A frown creased the brow at the mere mention of a chiropractor or holistic doctor—until now. Until Esther needed a miracle. A miracle like her dad experienced as a child.

ⓔⓔⓔ

An insidious epidemic of polio invaded Oklahoma City during the 1950's—the place of Seth's birth. When we first met, he told me about the successful, but unconventional methods used to cure him of polio as a child.

Seth explained, "At nine years old, I remember waking up with a headache and sore throat. I had a stiff neck with pain radiating into my back and I felt very weak and feverish. My mom suspected polio and immediately took me to Dr. Melson. He confirmed her suspicions and diagnosed me with bulbar poliomyelitis, a serious form of polio where the muscles used for swallowing, speaking, and breathing become paralyzed."

The most feared illness in the first half of the twentieth century, polio, a highly contagious viral disease, usually left its victims disabled, crippled or dead.

The only approved medical treatment at the time placed a child in an iron lung which administered prolonged artificial respiration by means of mechanical pumps.

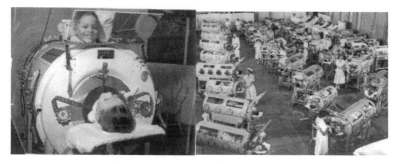

An Iron Lung   Polio epidemic

Seth's mother, an avid reader, knew reports of complete healing were rare, so she took him to Love's Chiropractic Center in Oklahoma City. Seth remained there for two weeks and received adjustments every few hours, underwent colon cleanses, and ate a special diet of vegetables, and fresh juices.

Over time, the treatments brought complete recovery with no side effects.

Seth's experience gave us reason to rethink how we should handle our family's health needs. We researched everything from the common cold to cancer (the most dreaded disease of *our* century) for the least invasive way to treat it.

Alternatives became the first preference for our family as long as they didn't endanger our well-being. We used antibiotics if needed, but we had a regimen of alternatives we tried first.

☉☉☉

My sister Katrina began choosing alternatives when she experienced twenty cancer deaths of friends and family within two years. Each had followed the standard medical route of surgery, radiation, chemo and drugs. This set her on a journey to find healthier ways to heal the body.

An avid researcher, over time, she collected a sizable library on alternative paths to healing cancer. She spoke to doctors, authors, and naturopaths world-wide. As she discovered alternate ways of healing the body of diseases, Katrina completely cured herself of severe Crohn's disease. She's now healthier and more energetic in her sixties than in her twenties.

Another friend beat ovarian cancer (usually a fatal diagnosis) using alternatives.

Over several years before Esther's cancer, Katrina shared her research with our family which we discussed often. Because of her information and our own personal study, we knew we'd make a better-informed decision if we were ever diagnosed with this dreaded disease.

Then—Esther's cancer diagnosis. She chose to leave chemo and radiation as a last resort.

ⓔⓔⓔ

Esther, Romeo, Seth and I met with the surgeon for Esther's post-surgery appointment. Stepping into this foreign world of cancer, we didn't even know what questions to ask. The pathology report said there were good margins with no cancer cells seen at the outer edge of the tissue or along the surrounding rim. Armed with this information seemed all the more reason to proceed with healthier therapies. But then like an earthquake, our family's postoperative consult with her surgeon, tilted our convictions as he boldly stated… "Without chemo and radiation, Esther *will* die!"

Esther asked, "What about patients who've used alternative treatments? What is their success rate?"

The doctor left no room for discussion when he stated, "*All* of them are dead, 100%!" Well, what could we say to that? We were already scared and traumatized, and at age twenty-six, death is unimaginable. The doctor came across with such authority. How do you come against that and discount what he said?

Upon hearing the doctor's report, Esther's Romeo, took up the chemo-radiation banner. Seth trusted the doctors over our limited knowledge of treating this specific cancer with alternatives. Seth and Romeo had never agreed on *anything*. Why this?

Esther, *not* on board with this treatment plan, wanted no part of beginning with chemo and radiation. The intense backlash of objections from family and friends took her by surprise. Raging contention spread over the landscape of her life. The pressure on Esther to comply with chemo-radiation *first* became ruthless and relentless.

Thoughts from Esther's Journal

I received a call from the hospital today about my PET scan and was told that the only place that "glowed" was the area of the surgery. (Only three weeks from surgery this area would naturally light up as it's still healing.) The cancer has NOT spread anywhere else in my body! Praise God! I am SO happy. I was praying yesterday and telling God that even if the cancer had spread everywhere, I will still trust Him. He is so faithful and kind. His mercies are new every morning. I am so thankful! Thank you for all your prayers. Thank you, thank you, thank you.

P.S. Please pray for guidance and wisdom as we make decisions about chemo, radiation, and second opinions.

Esther

The previous year of escalating pain, her recent surgery, a twenty-pound weight loss, and the backlash from not choosing chemo left her too physically and emotionally worn out to fight. It hurt to witness her struggle and inner turmoil. Needing peace, she chose to trust God to work through her husband and father; a positive attitude and inner calm were so critical.

With much at stake, because the chemo and radiation would destroy her reproductive organs, she said, "Marmie, I can't face chemo and the loss of my children too. I'll never make it through this."

Journal

I had an appointment with my reproductive biology doctor on Monday. She is absolutely amazing; I was impressed by her knowledge and wisdom. She did however confirm after going through chemo and radiation I would never be able to bear children. She did offer me hope though. If my oncologists will allow me to wait on beginning my chemo and radiation until October 1ˢᵗ, she would have enough time to grow and retrieve my eggs, make embryos, freeze them until we are ready to have babies, and then we will need a surrogate mother. It is overwhelming that I myself won't be able to bear children, but it is fascinating to think someone else can develop and bear my children. So, I will be on the lookout for a good, healthy friend to grow this precious little life. Please pray that everything will go well in the whole egg retrieval, embryo making process. Also, please pray that I will have high levels of estrogen during the treatments, as some very serious medical things will happen if I do not. Thank you again for all your prayers and words of kindness. You all lift me up, and are such a vital part of this, as it is not a war against flesh and blood. Thank you, dear prayer warriors, for fighting this unseen battle surrounding us.

Esther

Many people think alternative medical procedures are radical and unsubstantiated. Thankfully, from the acceptance of chiropractic care in the twenty-first century to the validity of alternatives such as Dr. Oz promotes today, people are waking up to healthier ways to treat disease.

The best alternative is *preventative* maintenance. Do your homework and be knowledgeable about how you would handle cancer. It becomes so emotional and overwhelming once you're in the middle of it.

I'm in no way giving medical advice, except to say, "Educate yourself". There are people who have come through chemo and are living full, active lives. But often with side-effects, and from my research, many don't survive.

Over the next three to four weeks Esther went through dozens of doctor appointments, scans and tests in preparation for her upcoming chemo and radiation. Mingled throughout these appointments were the complicated treatments to harvest eggs and shrink her reproductive organs to create a faux menopause. I cringed as I slid needles into her stomach for the necessary injections. Tear-stained pillowcases were evidence of this soul-crushing time.

In retrospect, the havoc the fertility treatments created were not worth it. It further weakened her immune system, and the chemo and radiation had not even begun. As much as I desired her children, I wanted *her* to come through the treatments alive and healthy.

Always on the lookout for some levity, we laughed when her fertility specialist announced, "Esther, you hold the record for the most eggs harvested in the Southeastern United States with a grand total of sixty-seven eggs. You've broken the previous record of forty-three!" The average harvest...a meager ten eggs. A definite "Fertile Myrtle," we celebrated the possibility of Esther's children and our grandchildren.

REFLECT

Right now, in the middle of your crisis of grief, are your personal resources enough? Have you prepared against tragedy but still ended up in a mess? How do you find relief from such devastating brokenness?

APPLY

In every crisis we have our own agenda and goal. If we only use man's wisdom, we'll fall short of God's higher purpose and plan. Life is full of missed ques and lost chances that seem so devastating to us, but God has a way of working all things together for our good and His glory.

Because we can't see the plan, we can become skeptical that God even knows what He's doing.

Read the riveting story of Joseph in Genesis chapters 37-50. Notice how in chapter 37 verses 1-2, 21, 27, God was *with* him and Joseph *knew* God was with him. In all of his rejection, betrayals, and anguish, God knew exactly what he was doing.

List the good things which came out of Joseph's suffering. Then journal God's possible purpose for your trial.

PRAYER

Dear Father God,

Like Joseph, I get ambushed and fall into a pit. Sometimes it's of my own making and other times it seems evil has the upper hand even though I'm trying so hard to do all the right things. Thank you for the story of Joseph. He had every reason to give up on your purpose for him yet he remained faithful through years of grueling labor, betrayals and disappointments. Solidify the same knowing in *my* heart, that you are *with* me and preparing me for an amazing future.

Chapter 6

The God of Surprises

A happy dance twirled in the midst of sorrows.

Mt. Everest-sized financial challenges had been on the horizon when I'd rushed Esther to the hospital for her original surgery in August 2010. Later we discovered the graphic design firm she worked for carried insurance which *covered* her *now* pre-existing cancer diagnosis. We'd never heard of an insurance company covering anything pre-existing and certainly not cancer, and so began a series of everyday miracles. Big or small, thankfulness became our *deliberate* mantra as we recognized our source.

"Every good and perfect gift is from above,

coming down from the Father of the heavenly lights. "

James 1:17

On earth we will have trouble. It's a fallen world. Unless we're aware God desires to reveal His love and grace within our dark nights, we might miss the gift wrapped within it. Be alert. Look for the beauty.

I lived an hour from Esther and with my teaching schedule, to take her to chemo and radiation appointments would take a minimum of three *driving* hours alone. Even if I cared for her part time, it would be hard to continue working.

Again, Esther's friend, Heidi, came along side to help. They'd become fast friends during high school. A mutual faith plus interest in art cemented their long term, soul-sister relationship.

At the time of Esther's cancer diagnosis, both she and Heidi were married and lived a thousand miles apart. Heidi's husband, Jeff, traveled frequently for business and could easily fly into town to be with her, and Heidi worked primarily from her computer. She offered to come and be Esther's caregiver during her three months of chemo and radiation. We are forever grateful for their sacrificial support. They were an answer to a prayer we didn't even know to pray for at the time.

I will answer them before they even call to me.

While they are still talking about their needs,

I will go ahead and answer their prayers.

Isaiah 65:24

Within two weeks of Esther's cancer diagnosis Seth and I celebrated our 40th wedding anniversary. My daughter, Jayne, and her husband, invited us to their home in Tennessee for a weekend to de-stress, process, and celebrate.

The first night, Seth and I lay in the guest room wailing out our pain and pent-up emotions. We held each other weeping from such a deep place, it seemed our internal organs would detach and spill. The thought of losing our dear girl seemed beyond endurance. I remember thinking, *how can I be in this much pain and still be alive?* We'd been through trials before, but nothing came close to this. We cried out to the Lord. We agonized in prayer.

Jayne and her husband gifted us with tickets for a sunset dinner cruise on the Tennessee River in Knoxville. The soft September breeze and spray of glistening water as the sun arched low sheathed us with peace. We savored a lovely meal and the sweetness of their well-timed gift.

☺☺☺

After two weeks of treatments, depression pressed in on Esther, (Never a good frame of mind while going through cancer.) Another everyday miracle arrived in the form of a weekend getaway to celebrate Romeo's birthday and their third wedding anniversary. Esther's boss sent them to his lake house for the weekend. Leaving doctors, needles, and drugs behind, the sunshine, autumn beauty, and gentle zephyrs off the lake renewed and encouraged them.

The following weekend, tickets to the Firebird ballet were provided for Esther and me from the parents of one of my piano students. Esther loved dance and it uplifted her spirits. (A huge thank you to ballet masters, Junuz and Gina Mazon, for their kindness and generosity).

The everyday miracles kept pouring in. A generous couple from our church offered their new luxury cabin called the Love Shack, in north Georgia, for a weekend in November. Heidi joined us as we created hand-made Christmas cards together. The Martins, a kindhearted family, blessed us many times with the gift of a healing getaway at their lovely bungalow.

These were some of the visible, hands-on blessings, but the prayers of people were consistent and powerful. A sense of well-being and peace would come at the oddest times. Many were praying for us throughout America and around the globe.

Slowly I learned soul-survival and a calm heart would only come from recognizing the Lord planned something much greater than I could understand. Accepting this, and giving thanks by faith, even in the clutches of heartbreak, would be my path to peace. God never failed to soothe my heart, but it required a moment by moment walk of faith. These God Surprises allowed me to *experience* the Lord's love through his people and His ever-present Spirit.

REFLECT

Are you staying alert and *looking* for the blessing within your trial? Has a complete stranger directed a smile your way? An inexplicable peace embraced you? A child's laughter delighted you?

APPLY

One time my granddaughter, Cassidy, spent the night and the next morning she came into the kitchen with a complaining, sour attitude. I sent her to her room to write out 10 things she felt thankful for. She returned and read me her list. Her whole countenance changed to smiles and surprise at her transformed attitude. Although that sounds simplistic to your crushing grief, a thankful heart for the small and big things can be one way *through* it.

* Read Anne Voskamp's book, "One Thousand Gifts."
* Listen to Mandesia's song, "A Broken Hallelujah."

PRAYER

Heavenly Father, in my grief, the last thing I want to do is give thanks. It's so much easier to swallow a pill, even for temporary relief. I realize man's medicine may be necessary too, but based on Your Word, I choose to look for ways to be thankful.

*Do not be anxious about anything, but in every situation by prayer and petition, **with thanksgiving**, present your requests to God. And the peace of God, which transcends all understanding, will guard your hearts and your minds in Christ Jesus.* (emphasis mine)

Philippians 4:6-7 NIV

Chapter 7

A Critical Delay

The intense reprimand from the nurse let Esther know she had been in a life-threatening crisis.

Three weeks of treatments left Esther withdrawn, struggling both physically and emotionally. Eating became an unpleasant chore as chemo altered her taste buds causing food to taste metallic or bland with no flavor.

Much more than submitting to chemo and radiation, Esther's sensitivity as a person, plus all the fertility treatments caused hormone imbalances and hot flashes creating an emotionally charged atmosphere. Burdens which added painful layers to her cancer.

Caring Bridge, an online site, allowed our family to update friends and family, relieving us from emotionally draining phone calls.

October 16, 2010

My Dearest Friends,

Thank you for constantly uplifting me in prayer. The enemy is hitting hard and I am in desperate need of your warrior hearts and words. God's word is my swift sword so please keep sending scripture for me to feast on. I'm feeling physically, emotionally, and spiritually weary today, but God is good and is ever faithful to me. He is going before me in a clear well-defined path.

Sustained by the Rock,

Esther

Monday, October 29th, found Esther back in the chemo clinic for an all-day session, ending with a trip to the radiologist. At home that evening, again nausea plagued her and food tasted like cardboard soaked in chemicals. At three a.m. Tuesday morning her temperature shot to 103 degrees. Too sick to realize her critical state, she didn't go to the emergency room until the next morning. She'd been instructed to seek immediate attention if her fever spiked. The previous harsh reaction of the head nurse *felt* mean, but only given to impress on Esther the seriousness of her and Romeo's lack of action.

Esther's journal...

The first week of chemo and radiation was dark and depressing. I hung by a thread. The third week I had an extremely high fever and almost died. My radiation

nurse, Tricia, told me Friday, the power of prayer must be holding me up because at this point in the treatment the strongest and toughest women come in crawling, brought to their knees because of the pain.

Friends from Esther's Bible study fasted and prayed for her. Her white blood count had plummeted, so all treatments were stopped. Esther remained at the cancer center all day receiving I.V. fluids and antibiotics. Possible exposure to infection at the hospital resulted in being sent home. Her temperature returned to normal after a couple of days of rest and her strength gradually returned.

I cleaned her house, washed clothes, and provided a much-appreciated gift for her missed wedding anniversary. I cleaned her piano which had been taken over by mice and boxes of online inventory from her husband's business and then had it tuned and put into pristine condition. Her smile, my reward.

ⓔⓔⓔ

Click-click-*shwerr*...papers rustled, computer keys tapped and printers hummed. The sounds of her workplace on Monday afternoon were music to Esther's ears where she worked as head of the design department. Stamina recovered and back at work, she only felt delight and surprise as she settled into her projects. She loved her job and had missed the whole previous week.

She'd spent the morning at a nurses' appointment for blood work. Her numbers weren't great but elevated enough to begin chemo again the next day.

Her overall treatment time from October through December 2013 was intense with lots of scary side-effects: blurred vision, mouth sores, continual nausea, and the ever-present fatigue and weight loss. Esther said the damage from the radiation was the worst part and wouldn't even talk about it. They'd given her mega treatments and explained her body would never tolerate it again.

Mingled throughout those weeks were many encouraging messages on her Caring Bridge website. Cards, flowers, meals, special getaway trips, and personal calls intertwined throughout, bringing much needed support. By Christmas her taste buds were coming back into alignment along with her appetite. Throughout the holidays we celebrated with local family. Long distance relatives and visitors came from as far away as the Ukraine.

After her last treatment, Esther posted a favorite poem, appreciating it with new insight:

I walked a mile with Pleasure, She chattered all the way;

But left me none the wiser, For all she had to say.

I walked a mile with Sorrow And ne'er a word said she;

But, oh, the things I learned from her

When Sorrow walked with me!

Robert Browning Hamilton

At her Bible Study Christmas Party, Esther was in awe as she and Romeo were presented a check for over $5,000 to help pay medical bills. This represented a huge sacrifice from these gracious people. A crowning blessing to the month of December!

REFLECT

Pondering Esther's poem, have you seen this contrast in your own life? The depth of character developed during your own crisis, compared to the shallowness in times of pleasure?

APPLY

Esther found ways to encourage and nurture herself through scripture, prayers, and reaching out to supportive friends. In similar ways, learn to love and nurture yourself also.

Personalizing scripture is a great way to undergird your heart and make scripture come alive. Read the following verse and say *your name* aloud to fill in the blanks.

John 17:23 NLT (Jesus prayer to The Father) "I am in_____, and You Father are in me. May _____ experience such perfect unity that the world will know that You "Father God" sent Me and that you love _____ as much as you love Me."

PRAYER

Dear Heavenly Father, its mind blowing to think you could love me just as much as you love your perfect Holy Son! Your ways are indescribable. Thank you for your crazy love.

Chapter 8

Celebration

With the last of chemo and radiation treatments in the rearview mirror, Esther soaked in the aromas and flavors of Christmas as she thought, *maybe* life could be good again.

January 2011, dawned new, bright and clean. Our whole family longed for a new beginning of *good* reports, but no one more than Esther.

An appointment with her oncologist the end of January left her heart filled with song as he reported, "Everything looks good! You're recovering well!"

Still, ongoing fatigue, hot flashes, and first-time acne from her fertility treatments dogged her days, but her red blood cell count returned to a normal range. With a CAT scan ordered, her sights focused on a fresh start with new hope.

My January birthday landed on a Saturday, so Esther and I decided to make it a Celebration Tea Party of her successful journey back to health. What better gift could I ask for? Esther sent special hand-made invitations to several longtime friends who had been so supportive during her illness.

Ideas of fancy delicacies danced in our heads as we polished miniature silver spoons and washed special plates, fancy bone-china teacups, saucers, and teapots. Our happy hearts performed dainty pirouettes of joy. We planned special petite sandwiches of pimento cheese and chicken salad—crusts removed of course. Cranberry-orange scones with clotted cream and plain scones with tongue-tingling lemon curd to entice the most particular palate. Special homemade freezer jams provided the crowning touch.

From our collection of special teas, we chose some favorites: English Breakfast, Lavender Earl Grey, and Peaches and Cream.

Esther designed the invitations announcing *only* the celebration of the completion of her treatments—or so I thought. When ladies started showing up with birthday gifts, I knew she'd slipped one past me. The delight of her duplicity lit up her face. Her endearing quality of celebrating others surfaced and blessed me.

I would be remiss not to mention how the blessings continued to pour down on our dear girl, and therefore, on our hearts as well. In February, the parents of her friend Heidi sent Esther and Romeo on an all-expense paid trip to Miami and a cruise to the Bahamas. We are forever grateful to them for this over-the-top generous gift. The *best* news came the end of March 2011 when Esther's oncologist reported, "You're CANCER FREE!

REFLECT

Have you ever noticed it's *after* a storm when you see the most beautiful Sunrises or Sunsets?

APPLY

Sometimes a storm guts us and alters our life forever— maybe like the event which caused you to pick up this book? Esther's faith and life purpose were already set in place before her cancer. Her spiritual growth and influence in the next years embedded the footprints of Jesus across many more hearts. Allow her story to compel you to set your life purpose with an eye toward the eternal.

PRAYER

Dear Father God,

Your minister of grace, the apostle Paul, begged you to take away an unrevealed personal infirmity three times. Your response: "My grace is all you need. My power works best in weakness." 2 Corinthians 12:9 NLT

May you use me, a weakened vessel, to first know you and understand the depth of your love for me and the grace you want to provide in this trial. May I be a vessel of your love to others.

Chapter 9

A Test of Faith

Doctors, needles, and tests were history as Esther embraced the brighter future ahead. She settled into the work she loved at her flourishing graphic design business. The only designer when hired, she'd worked hard to brand the company as a first-class design firm. She was not only an exceptional artist and creator, but also a skilled businesswoman—likable and easy to work with. The company had thrived, but like a thick mist cloaking danger, change hovered in the air.

Like a dam with a threatening leak, Esther felt weakened both physically and professionally as she lost the management position of the department she had created. Since she'd been in and out of work with her cancer treatments, a young new graphic designer stepped into her role as the head of creative design.

In time, Esther proved herself and was offered the Art Director's position again. She said "Yes" to the offer but then struggled as she worked through all its ramifications. Only a few months since she'd finished her cancer treatments, she knew the position wasn't worth the price of her health. Longer hours and more responsibilities caused her to rethink her decision. Hiring and firing employees and the stress as a department head required a tough hide.

Romeo's coercion to take the position for health insurance and increased income influenced her decision. Her passionate desire to own a home compelled her to accept and add a major free-lance project as well.

November 2011

I dream of living on Willow Lane. Waking with the sun, my journal and cup of hot tea in my hands on a quiet screened-in-porch. Giving my beginning moments to Him who made me. Letting the dogs out into the expansive fenced yard covered with the leafy branches of large old trees. A little white picket fence around our kitchen garden and a wood-chipped covered path winding through our property. I would design and write in my personal office in the morning, house cleaning and projects in the afternoon. Prepare a delicious candle-lit dinner for us with a glass of wine on the back screened-in porch. A simple bath and book to end the day.

As she expected, her position required more and more stamina as the company grew, but her workplace soon became oppressive. Still, her desire to own a home drove her forward, so she persevered and bloomed in her present circumstance.

Father God, there is so much on my mind, and amazingly you give me peace in the midst of it. Trying to prove I can lead a department is difficult. They see me as being kind and soft spoken. They know not the warrior within that has fought many battles of the soul, body, and spirit.

I'm letting go of perfect, and hanging on to you, Lord.

More changes occurred when her boss and owner of the company struggled with personal issues and hired a new manager for daily operations.

With the new leader in place, the owner became much less involved with the business. Without delay his intense disgust for women in leadership positions revealed itself. Esther, along with other women in the company, felt the sting of his bigoted views but targeted Esther for his harshest treatment.

Late November 2011

I want to scream at the top of my lungs. I am working so hard and feel as though it never ends and I'm not being paid accordingly. I am being taken advantage of, and it makes me so angry...I'm so tired and am having a serious meltdown...I don't want to be ungrateful for my job. I just feel extremely offended, frustrated, and underpaid. Enough is enough!

Today my heart sank as I realized I must continue to work underpaid, overworked, and understaffed. I want to give up, to scream, to cry. I am exhausted and to know this will continue through Christmas—well, it's beyond disheartening.

She closed with...

Sing and make music in your heart to the Lord. Always giving thanks to God the Father for everything.

God—her comforter, her rock and shield.

As the year of 2011 progressed, so did the managers degree of scorn for Esther.

March 2012

Looking at a situation at work over the past two days, it is clear Al is not changing...his discrimination against me, it is worse."

I woke early, my restless mind churning with office politics—wondering if it's worth facing off with Al.

Like a predator setting up his quarry for the kill, the new manager's diabolical injustice became so obvious, other employees challenged him: "Either stop tormenting Esther, or let her go. This is beyond painful to watch!"

Then, Esther's co-worker and closest friend resigned. This created a huge vacuum of support for Esther as she struggled with the continued onslaught of her bosses bullying.

Financial problems had been an earmark in Esther's life since her marriage, so the following day when she found Romeo had drained their savings account, it felt like acid in an open wound.

I have been deeply betrayed, and my heart is broken. I don't know where to go from here. He doesn't see it as a big deal, and that's what worries me. What he vowed never to do; he has done.

Her hope for a home and need for a less stressful job felt out of reach.

My job is wearing hard on my health. The stress is very high. I used to love my job, but it is time to leave and bring balance to my marriage.

April 2012

Spring is in full bloom. Showers of white cherry blossoms and happy songbirds. A melancholy heart in the midst of spring is ridiculous. How can my heart ache as the cherry trees dance in the sunlight? As triumphant daffodils rise from the dead of winter? I am momentarily stung again and I feel frozen. Hands tied. My stomach turns as the sweet breeze caresses my face. He is my beloved, my heart's only...why does he choose to hurt me so deeply again?

Life seemed to be caving in on Esther from all directions, but her next words were full of hope as she stood strong in her faith.

Thank you for working in me Father God; removing the clutter and debris from my life. It is indeed impossible for me to have a need you cannot meet. You are sovereign. May I see the everlasting invisible through your eyes. Thank you for suffering in the deepest way for me, for setting me free. May my heart always be thankful.

I've been trying to ignore it, but lately, I have not been feeling well—similar to how I felt before I discovered I had cancer. I feel a disturbing sickness grab my whole body, especially a tension in my stomach and insides so I feel too weak to even move. Today it happened again and dug up some horrific memories bringing instant tears to my heart and eyes.

May 2012

Today a huge battle was waged against me. It began when Al told me I must move out of my office into the open to make room for a new sales manager. There are two men who do not manage anyone who are keeping their offices. It was insult to injury...enough discriminations. I cried in front of Al as I told him I was taking the rest of the day off...so humiliating. I feel like I failed so many times today.

The devotional 'Jesus Calling' spoke right into the situation. 'Everything I endure can be put to good use by allowing it to train me in trusting you. This is how I foil the works of evil, growing grace through the very adversity meant to harm me.' Father, I claim this truth over my difficult circumstance. You are my provider, the one whose love casts out fear. The Chain-Breaker, the Sovereign One.

Father, this day looms before me and I really don't want to go to work. I am exhausted from the week-long battle, but you are mighty to save. May my weakness open me up to your power. The new sales manager is creepy and slick. He spoke down to me yesterday, telling me how to design, calling me sweetie and touching my arm. I don't want to lash out...but I won't be walked over...give me your balance of truth and love.

Esther was moved from her private office to an open non-management area. When she confronted the owner about the injustice, he said, "It's no big deal, and I'm disappointed in your reaction." Loss of respect was immediate as co-workers asked her: "Have you been demoted?"

She pasted a visual in her journal of a woman deteriorating which revealed her soul. No big deal?

Romeo treated Esther to a weekend out of town. A good movie and scrumptious dinner helped her rejuvenate and relax. How I wish he could have seen the reality of what the stress was doing to her—body and soul.

June 2012

In my mind, I should have quit my job weeks ago, yet every day I go back out of respect for my husband's concern regarding our health insurance.

Esther was not a drama queen, but her worst and best characteristic was the willingness to absorb other's pain and even wrongs done to her. She desired to honor and love others well. But according to I Timothy 5:8, a man who does not provide for his own household has denied the faith and is worse than an infidel. Esther's choice to carry the heavy financial load enabled Romeo's disfunction as a provider and compromised her health. God grows us through our trials, but her choices were misaligned. As I read her journals and realized the intense layers of personal pain she dealt with on the job and at home, it became clear why she hadn't regained her physical strength and stamina from her previous cancer.

☺☺☺

In the process of my cancer research, I stumbled onto the answer of my question: "Why do some people who live a healthy lifestyle end up with cancer, and others who don't, sail through life just fine?"

A clinical study attempted to answer that question. A large group of cancer patients were interviewed. They found 90% of the patients had experienced traumatic events within 3 to 5 years of their cancer diagnosis. High stress suppresses the immune system and increases the possibility of disease. It did not take a psychic to guess Esther's future.

ⓔⓔⓔ

Esther's date to leave her job kept being pushed forward as it was important to keep her insurance coverage considering her history of cancer. Romeo's online business experienced two crashes, and his part-time soccer coaching job was lost just when it should have been soaring.

Our family never understood Romeo's reasons for not pursuing a full-time position with benefits in order to take care of Esther. He was brilliant, with many skills, and seemed to work hard at what he did.

When the nearby university built their state-of-the-art women's athletic field, Esther and our family urged him to apply for a lead coaching position and utilize his expertise in this field. Esther had connections which might have helped. He refused. I asked him, "Why?" He said, "It's not that easy. It's complicated." After ten years of observation, I concluded he purposely stayed below-the-radar. Perhaps he didn't want to leave a paper trail? To *me*, it seemed he was hiding.

Yet in the midst of such stress and loss, Esther's faith became a palpable reality and she radiated a supernatural light. I wish you, the reader, could sit with her journals as I have and see pages covered with artwork, scriptures, praise songs, and words of thankfulness, regardless of what she was going through. Like King David who wrote most of the Psalms, she would cry out, rant, weep over injustice, then surrender and melt into the secure arms of her God. A peaceful place to land.

Her life, a mosaic of broken fragile glass, sparkled in the Son's light and became a masterpiece. Over the next three years, her glow would penetrate a chasm of great darkness.

For we are God's masterpiece.

He has created us anew in Christ Jesus,

so we can do the good things he planned for us long ago.

Ephesians 2:10 NLT

REFLECT

Do you realize Jesus desires to create a masterpiece of you? The Japanese are known for a centuries old art called Kintsugi, where they repair broken pottery with a special lacquer dusted with powdered gold, silver or platinum. The broken pottery becomes more beautiful than in its original state and *much* more valuable.

APPLY

If you're grief is fresh, you may only see the broken shards of brittle, ugly clay right now. Hang in there my fellow-warrior. Trust God with all your broken pieces and watch Him transform them into splendor.

- Memorize Eph 2:10 so you'll remember *you* are His masterpiece.
- Listen to the song, "Masterpiece," by Danny Gokey

PRAYER

Dear Heavenly Father, hang on to me or I won't make it out of this quagmire of pain and sorrow. When it tries to suck me under, I choose now to lay the fragments of my anguish into your skilled, nail-scarred palms. Let my life reflect the touch of Your masterful hand.

Chapter 10

A Creative Renaissance

A Creative Renaissance is a process of rebirth. It's exciting, but takes time and requires patience. Esther *would* leave her present workplace, but when? Change plus hope glowed strong as multiple possibilities tumbled into her life.

March 2013

I just ran into a client from Dark2Light Printing who works at a ministry for men who are working through alcohol and drug addictions. They broker print jobs with our design firm occasionally. He offered me a job to come work for them as a designer. He said it would be a lot less money, but much more fun. They are transitioning to be completely design-centered. Hmm... might be just my thing. Ministry centered design. I like it. Father, may I be attentive to your voice. Is this part of your agenda?

This one-year in-house program for men addicted to drugs and alcohol, became a flickering candle of hope in the darkness of Esther's present life-draining employment.

Yet, in the light of her current financial and insurance circumstances, accepting the offer seemed impossible. As with many non-profit ministries, the *less income* her client referred to, meant she had to raise her own salary. But she knew what's impossible with man, God loves to birth into reality.

Another possibility came in the form of an invitation to move to Tennessee near her sister, Jayne, and create a family farm. The thought of multiple lakes and waterways with mountain backdrops, the wildlife and peaceful quiet, brought visions of body and soul-renewal, a place to call home. Although tempting, personal family dynamics gave her pause.

An additional door opened when Romeo applied for a position at a Military College, two hours away. Leaving family and friends behind would be hard, but to leave her present job became Esther's primary goal. They found an affordable house in the college town and Esther's creative juices flowed as she envisioned an Art Nouveau décor. Her dreams of freedom were squashed again when Romeo was not hired.

August 2013

I felt as though someone took the key to my cell and threw it into the abyss!

Esther seemed to be doing all the right things. She recognized and stood up for her right as a child of God to be equal to a man in value. Wise enough to move on to find new employment when it was obvious Al was not going to change. She continued to submit to God in the process, but *why* couldn't she get a break?

August 2013

After my deep soul-bearing talk with my Lord in the early hours before dawn...I surrendered all to him: Continuing to work at my present job, hope of a home, hope of a child, and a balanced marriage. A wonderful lifting of my burdens and an all-encompassing peace began to reside in my soul. Thank you for your faithfulness, Oh God, even when I scream, kick, and complain. You reach out your gracious hand of hope and compassion, even as I've been going through this 'time of the closed door'.

I often noticed in my own life, when I finally surrender *my* way, *my* stuff, *my*_____, fill in the blank, God would show up. It's amazing how quickly things can change.

A few days later...

September 2013

When I saw the Dark2Light website and video on Monday afternoon, it triggered something in me, an invitation to tour and possibly work there. So, I am taking Edward up on this and will tour today at 11 a.m. and see what their ministry is all about. To you Father God be the Glory.

My tour went well yesterday, a brightness resides there. They are about to launch a new marketing campaign and are looking for experienced designers to add a new level of expertise to their business and ministry. I deeply desire to do graphic design for a ministry and

Romeo is against it as it doesn't bring in much money. Father, you have cleared the way towards Dark2Light, only you can clear Romeo's mind.

Romeo and his mom are so desperate for me to stay in the corporate world, yet my heart, soul, mind, and body are ready to use my gifts and talents for your ministry, Lord. It is time. I long to be on your path.
Amen.

"...sorrowful yet always rejoicing; poor, yet making many rich; having nothing, and yet possessing everything."

II Corinthians 6:10 NIV

Father, thank you for teaching me more intimately about my spiritual armor, especially my breastplate of righteousness. Only by truly accepting the robe of righteousness you purchased with your blood, can I truly protect my heart. May I walk with a humble and thankful heart as I wear my glorious robe. As my worship of you has grown deeper, I have discovered a new dimension of intercessory prayer in the midst of my praise to you. What treasures and jewels you are revealing to me. Thank You! You showed me in the early hours a couple of days ago, the possibilities of a home with the help of Dark2Light. After I shared this with Romeo, he seemed more receptive to going on a tour there!

Wait patiently for the LORD.

Be brave and courageous.

Yes, wait patiently for the LORD.

Psalm 27:14 NLT

REFLECT

Like Esther, are your circumstances placing you in what seems like a prison cell? You may be thinking, *'the verse above makes me angry! I'm in a life and death situation here! I'm in so much emotional pain I can't even process my thoughts. Patience? Ahhh... you may be saying, my patience meter is minus 10 and continues falling!*

APPLY

Many main characters in great stories are brought to a place of such dire need, hopelessness, and tension first; then, the redemptive situation or deliverer can be revealed with the greatest impact to bring change. Patience is a big part of the progression. In real life, *you* are the main character. It is to this place God is trying to bring you.

But those who wait on the LORD shall renew their strength; they shall mount up with wings like eagles, they shall run and not be weary, they shall walk and not faint.
Isaiah 40:31 NKJV

PRAYER

I bow Father, and in my impatient desire for relief from my present painful circumstances, I choose surrender, I choose life, I will trust You.

Chapter 11

Dark 2 Light

August melted into September's azure skies with shorter days and cooler nights. Romeo's heart opened to the possibilities of Esther joining Dark 2 Light, but raising funds to create Esther's personal salary seemed awkward and daunting. She felt uncomfortable asking people for their hard-earned resources. Although a definite leap of faith, she took the challenge with her usual resolve and grit. Ready to plunge into the deep as she placed her confidence in her Papa God—her provider. As she remembered His past faithfulness, her discomfort turned to peace.

September 2013

Father, it is amazing to look back and see how much you've grown, refined and molded me. Dreams and wishes turned into prayers and hopes. You are sovereign!

Considering her present circumstances, the name Dark2Light, seemed prophetic. She sensed an oasis on the horizon when Romeo agreed to visit the campus.

They toured the grounds which consisted of several businesses besides the print and design center where Esther would provide graphic design training for the men.

I cannot believe this is happening. We had a great meeting with the founder. Romeo's concerns for my safety, (due to the possible behaviors of clients dealing with addictions) ...were kindly met with comforting answers...98% improbability that anyone would ever lash out or harm me.

More good news! I would have health and dental insurance. They will pay for 80% of my monthly payment—so instead of $1,000 a month, I would pay $160!

Hallelujah!! Romeo and I are on the same page and I will leave my soul-draining job and begin work on November 8th!

Esther's journal relates her meeting with two leaders for lunch the next day to work on the intimidating process of raising her own salary. Over the next few days, her letters were written, prayed over, and put in the mail to perspective supporters.

After all the waiting and persecution, it is difficult to believe... WOW! Thank you, Father, for your amazing work in my and Romeo's heart...I am truly honored that you have opened the door for me. Deep calls unto deep. November 8th, I will be...Walking in light! Who says you don't have a sense of humor?

REFLECT

When have you been in a trial and felt gagged and bound? Have you ever been in a situation where you couldn't see a way out? Blocked by a key person who's not likely to alter their course or opinion? Maybe you're in a prison of your own making?

APPLY

Esther had no supernatural powers. Clay feet were her lot the same as you and me. She *chose* humility over self-rule, turning her dreams and desires into prayers, and overcoming fear through songs of praise. Take a moment and physically write out your areas of pride, your dreams, your fears. Now turn them over to the only one who's shoulders are big enough to handle them and carry you to victory. Through the cross, Jesus has already won your freedom. Claim it.

PRAYER

Dear Sovereign Father, lover of my obstinate, proud, and fearful heart. I purposely examine my ways, and with open hands I choose to let *You* carry me. Direct my paths and cover me with your peace.

Chapter 12

Bound No Longer

The cruel harassment toward Esther intensified throughout her last month, but also created a granite-edged-determination to finish well.

October 2013

I will not give in. My God is stronger and His ways are higher than any other. He is AWESOME in power... I will have joy, even in my most difficult day.

Esther stepped into the office of the owner and CEO of her present employment. She struggled internally but breathed a prayer to speak truth in love as she resigned her position as Creative Art Director. Once she began, words flowed like a gel-inked pen over glossy paper.

A couple of days later Esther still felt the sting of rejection as she'd held on to a grain of hope and thought, *maybe someone will acknowledge all the hard work I've done.* It didn't happen.

Leaving my bare desk which is no longer mine...I realized I no longer work here. Although bittersweet, it felt good to shake the dust from my feet and walk out the door.

That evening as she wrote in her journal, a faithful God provided a special affirmation to her day.

Wow, I found this verse by accident when I was reading my devotional.

"By faith Abraham, when called to go to a place he would later receive as his inheritance,

Obeyed and went.,

even though he did not know where he was going."

Hebrews 11:8

As I wrote it here in my journal, I realized the verse location 11:8 is my start date at Dark 2 Light. God, you are amazing!

I'm so encouraged.

REFLECT

Are you determined to finish well? Is your God stronger? Will you choose joy?

APPLY

Find God's power in Worship Songs. Our enemy hates our Worship of God and he will flee.

Raise your voice in a song of worship. If you don't sing, speak them aloud.

On You Tube listen to Chris Tomlin's powerful words put to a simple melody.

Our God

Our God is greater, our God is stronger
God you are higher than any other
Our God is healer, awesome in power
Our God, Our God

PRAYER

Heavenly Father,

The world-wide changes because of the Coronavirus pandemic are scaring me. In fact, I don't even want to think about what it could mean for my future, my family, and the world.

As I listened to the song *Our God*, I realize I've never been in a place like this, where my faith is and will be tested. But if I believe the words to Chris Tomlins song and you can open the eyes of the blind and shine into my darkness, I **will** arise from the ashes. You conquered death *for* me. It's not about my good works, is it? That kind of thinking depends on my performance. My heart can stay calm and confident from the fear of death. Live or die, in You, I win.

Chapter 13

Abundance and Favor

A vivid dream prompted Esther to e-mail the following account to me.

November 2013

With eyes barely opened, dim light filtered in around the edges of the drapes. I heard muffled voices, soft footfalls, and sounds of a suitcase rolling down the hotel hallway outside my door. I dozed again into a light slumber.

Something fell and sharp edges scraped the back of my hand. Startled, I stumbled to the bathroom, rinsed the blood away from the three claw-like scratches and searched for a bandage. Finding none, I wrapped my hand in a towel, slipped into my robe, and made my way to the elevator. Maybe someone at the front desk could help.

As I walked, I started finding money on the floor. At first a dollar, then three one-dollar bills rolled up. Some I picked up and put in my pocket, but if someone was close by, I gave them the money. Later I found five-dollar bills and eventually tens and twenties. Some alone, others rolled together. In my heart, they felt like little gifts to me from above, overflowing more and more.

Abruptly, I woke and thought it was Monday. Then I realized, 'No, this is Sunday my day of rest.' I snuggled back under the covers.

Her first days at Dark 2 Light confirmed her dream to be prophetic.

"Marmie, Romeo took me to work this morning and as we parked in front of the Studio, our eyes met and like a veil lifting, I could see the reality of our decision hit him. Like, *what have we done? How did I ever agree to this?* His agreement for me to work here had amazed me." She chuckled, "I think maybe God blocked out his male logic and reasoning to bring me to this place. It's such a miracle."

The king's heart is like a stream of water directed by the LORD; he guides it wherever he pleases.

Proverbs 21:1 NLT

Friday marked the completion of Esther's first week. To celebrate, we went to our favorite Italian restaurant. In a dither of playfulness, Esther wriggled in her seat. Delight lit her face and colored her voice.

"Oh, Marmie! I know I already told you about my dream..."

I nodded and interrupted, "Yes, but I'm puzzled about the scratches on your hand in your dream. What were they about?"

"Yes, I wondered too. I think it represented my time at my old job. I used my hands to create and design for them and had been so wounded. My time there started peaceful, even wonderful, then became so painful I had to leave."

"Hmm, I can see—"

"But wait 'til you hear about the rest of my week," she interrupted. A blush of excitement tinted her cheeks. "The first of the week I received a large box of donated groceries, but it's not like you'd think. Marmie, amazing food filled my counter as I unpacked it. Pricey, healthy, Trader-Joe type meals. Even with my previous income, I would never have considered it affordable."

"Sounds wonderful..."

"But wait! I'm just getting started. Tuesday, I visited my spot of guilty pleasures."

I had no idea where this was going, I grinned and waited.

"The Dutch Monkey Doughnut Shop!"

I laughed, "That's a new one to me."

"The owners know me, so when I told them I now worked for Dark 2 Light, they packed a large box with delectable treats of their fresh daily, from-scratch-donuts, and gifted them to me. Dark 2 Light has a great reputation in the community."

"Good to hear."

"Then," she gushed, "Wednesday, Romeo's car wouldn't start and men from the ministry came, towed it to the shop and fixed it. They only charged for the discounted parts."

"Wow! That's amazing honey." I began to bobble with excitement in my own chair.

"A realtor we'd been working with became *so* excited to hear about the ministry, she gave us a house!"

I choked on my pear-walnut salad as I coughed and sputtered... "WHAAT?!"

I thought she would tumble from her seat as she whooped, "Just kidding, Marmie, but the men from Dark 2 Light *do* attend the realtor's church."

In our minds, these events were designed by the *Master* engineer.

My mother's heart did a hallelujah-jig.

Esther's creative renaissance had come through a long painful labor and its birth was like a rare flower opening into breath-taking beauty.

Her first day at her new job, lyrics of a worship song scrolled across her journal...

November 2013

"Our God is greater, our God is stronger, God you are higher than any other!"

I feel so free, free to be myself, to share God's work in my life, free to live, to enjoy. I am SO blessed. Wow!

I am starting to get excited about how God is going to use me. It's so good to be out of the valley and walking in the rolling hills of providence and favor. Thank You, Father, all praise to you, Oh Mighty God. I was singing praises last night under the night sky on our back patio, and as I gazed up singing, a beautiful meteor shot across the darkness. Thank you, Father, for speaking hope to me through your creation.

Light wind, warm sun, loveliness of fall surrounds me as I sit on my blanket in the grass. A tree with autumn berries towers on one side and another nearby is on fire with golden yellows, oranges, greens, browns, and reds! Father, thank you for this moment of peace and tranquility in my day.

Father, your thumbprint on me is creativity, encouragement, the heart of an artist, love of nature, an appreciation of heritage and antiquity, yet a love for the elegance of modernity, a peacemaker with a passion for family ties, an imagination that dreams and sees visions and hopes for more.

It's not a TGIF day anymore, but an ILTBH day, as in I Love to Be Here Day. I'm so very happy. Truly a time of abundance! I have men who make me lunch every day and I have groceries I never would be able to afford, so many donations of goods.

Before long, Esther's love for art and fine teas steeped into the lives of the staff—even to the manliest of men.

REFLECT

How did Esther's actions remove grief from her life in her present circumstance? What are your resources when life tramples *your* heart?

APPLY

The ugly truth is—in this life, we're either going into a trial, in between trials, or coming out of one. We're going to be constantly disappointed with life if we think we're promised heaven-on-earth. The truth is, we live in a *war zone*. A few years ago, the powerful movie, "The War Room" was released. Use this resource to help you fight back. You don't have to remain in grief.

PRAYER

Dear Father of peace and healed hearts, I need You! I've experienced fear, betrayals, and disappointment in people. My soul screams out the legitimate *whys* of pain, death, and suffering too. Yet, I'm beginning to see Your faithfulness within it, *and* recognize it's a process and takes time. Like Esther, use my pain to comfort others. Turn my ashes into glory.

Chapter 14

Walking by Faith

Fear crept in as Esther prepared to teach her first class.

Creativity in designing for clients versus teaching in a classroom were very different. Creating a design syllabus from the foundation of ancient hieroglyphics to the present forms and mediums of design, proved quite the challenge.

November 2013

There is such talent at Dark 2 Light and I feel they have such high expectations of me.

My stomach is in knots as I prepare for my first lesson today. It seems silly, but I want so much for it to go well. Father, these anxious thoughts aren't from you, please let them melt away in the light of your loving presence.

Smiles all around validated her well-prepared lesson. She continued to teach all the aspects of design, composition, components of shape, typography as she created a 200-page syllabus.

The men under her training, would be prepared for employment opportunities when they graduated from her course. What a beautiful thing.

I'll never forget our conversation after she'd experienced teaching for a few days.

"Mom, I can't believe how much I love teaching. I'm finding it is so fulfilling and I'm shocked by this!"

As a music educator—I totally got it. We laughed and reveled in her new-found passion.

A short time later, Seth and I visited the campus. As we bounced down the long gravel driveway, visually nothing was inviting or awe-inspiring. But, like a saber cutting through earth's ordinary, when I opened the car door and placed my foot on the ground, I felt I'd entered Narnia; an imaginary place of wonder covered with peace. The ministries nestled here were consistently covered by prayer which explained the tranquil atmosphere. I felt it then and in every future visit. Esther, in a safe environment and creatively fulfilled, had landed right where she belonged.

The dream of abundance continued. Unexpected checks, a client insisted on paying Esther even though she explained her work was complimentary. Then a bonus Christmas check, a Starbucks card, gas for her car, invitations to dinners, a free Chick-fil-A lunch, and the list continued to expand.

@ @ @

As Esther learned to walk by faith in the Lord's provision of her physical needs, a sweet story emerged. The spring of 2014 her love of the outdoors led her into some horticulture projects. Visions of mouth-watering juicy tomatoes lured her to try gardening. She bought some plants and snuggled them into the newly broken sod in her yard. Then she realized tomato stakes would be necessary to support them. Not finding any makeshift materials to use, she sent up a quick sincere prayer. "Lord, I need some tomato stakes."

Riding along with a good friend two days later on a shopping errand, the driver suddenly jerked the car into the oncoming lane, barely missing some debris on the road. Excited, Esther squealed, "Stop the car! Pull over and back up. Look—there's my tomato stakes!"

Her friend thought she'd lost it—but sprawled across the road were long spikes of wood. As she loaded the trunk with the splintery wooden jewels, she giggled like a child at Christmas, thanking her Jehovah-Jireh, *The God who provides.*

Her friend, Vera, also provided her with tomato seeds straight from her home country. Heirloom seeds produce plants with consistent traits and offer an intense flavor putting them in a class of their own. Her plants produced such an abundance of flavorful tomatoes, her landlord took over the garden space thinking her tasty harvest was from the soil.

REFLECT

Did you know God is so crazy in love with you he not only knows when you need insignificant tomato stakes, but he knows how many hairs are on your head at any given moment? Who else in the world even cares? Every speck of information in your DNA is known to Him.

Hebrews 11:6 NIV

And without faith it is impossible to please God,
because anyone who comes to him
must believe that he exists
and that he rewards those who earnestly seek him.

APPLY

Nestle these words from Hebrews close to your heart. God cares about the smallest details in your life—even growing happy healthy tomatoes. When we ask in simple childlike faith within what He knows is good for us, he can't resist.

PRAYER

Heavenly Father, even though I walk in shadows of sadness and fear in my present pain, by faith I *will* take comfort in the knowledge of your care. Your provision for me is worth so much more than a bushel of tomatoes.

Chapter 15

Snow Globe Wonder

Not long after Esther started work at Dark 2 Light our whole family met at our daughter Jayne's for Thanksgiving 2013. It seemed to be a good idea. We loved each other, but the family was unraveling. Anticipating the holiday, Esther had prayed fervently over our time together. Her journaled prayer:

Paint our family portrait, Lord.

Let us be your Masterpiece.

Thank you for not giving up on us.

Yet, relationships seemed to hit bottom with no hope: a marriage unraveled, a child felt responsible, and other strained parent-child relationships threatened to capsize. Trusting God to overcome, Esther and I spent time together Sunday morning and asked God for a miracle.

The same day, Jayne suggested a round table discussion, but then backed out. Esther said, "No! We're doing this!" Then she laid out some ground rules. Sunday afternoon we came together at the kitchen table to have an honest, open discussion. As truthful sharing took place, tears flowed, and a great healing occurred within the core of our family. We knew we were witnessing a miracle as a sweet peace settled over us.

The LORD hears his people

when they call to him for help.

He rescues them from all their troubles.

Psalm 34:17 NIV

The healing in our family at Thanksgiving prompted Esther and Romeo to use their timeshare points to give our whole family a Christmas gift of five days at Sea Glass Tower in Myrtle Beach, South Carolina. Each family had their own room with floor-to-ceiling glass walls. What a special time with an amazing view. Great memories to hold forever in our hearts.

December 2013

I awoke slowly today as I gazed out these windowed walls and saw the sun rise and transform into so many shapes and colors, I even saw dolphins gliding over the ocean on their merry way.

Special family moments were sprinkled throughout the five days of our stay. The most precious gift to Esther was when her fifteen-year-old niece, Cassidy, told Esther she wanted to be the surrogate mother of her child someday.

Cassi gave me a paperweight of silver that said 'Hope.' Her offer to be my surrogate filled me with fresh 'hope' in the fulfillment of God's promise to me for a son. So, this gift is very symbolic. Thank you, God, for the kind loving heart of Cassidy.

Like standing inside a snow globe, December 26th found us in awe. We were encased by the resorts glass-walls watching fluffy cotton-ball-sized snowflakes float to earth. Our vehicles were under a downy blanket of thick chilly wool as we packed to head home.

A beautiful ending to a Christmas of priceless memories.

REFLECT

Have you ever had an honest conversation with a family member or your family as a whole? It's one of the hardest discussions in this life, right? Did they engage with you? Were they receptive to your insights or questions? Did you try working with a counselor or mediator?

APPLY

Tragedy can push us out of our comfort zones and bring out emotions we didn't know we were capable of. Very few are willing to pay the personal price to break their family's generational sin. It's *especially* hard with family members as that's usually where our original wounding takes place. The first step to healing is to deal with your own emotional injuries and bathe the whole process in prayer. This primary foundation of life is worth fighting for!

- Check out Andy Stanley's series "The Fight Club" on YouTube.

PRAYER

Father, Your Word says, "What's impossible with man, is possible with You." Luke 18:27

No matter how long it takes, please bring healing to my family. Create the stunning work of your grace and beauty into our lives.

Chapter 16

Abrams Creek

The ancient lofty trees, moist breezes, and whiffs of wood smoke washed my soul clean of big city stress and tensions. Gentle ripples of a nearby pristine creek sparkled like diamonds haphazardly flung across the water. My squinting eyes responded to the brightness as sounds of children's laughter absorbed into the canvas of temporary shelters.

Although a lovely setting, the fact remained, camping is labor intensive. My daughter, Jayne, worked hard as she planned these days of delightful fun and relaxation for our tribe. She and her family lived in the country on a small farm.

A short twenty-minute drive from her home lay the outskirts of the Great Smoky Mountain National Park, where a little-known campground nestled alongside Abram's Creek.

Jayne and her husband, Paul, set up tents and hauled in the one-thousand plus items to create a semblance of home away from home. The spacious campsites created a feeling of privacy even though a bit primitive. Bathrooms were provided but no hot water or showers. Other amenities included a fire pit, water spigot and large picnic table. Echoes of a small gurgling waterfall upstream provided sound therapy and white noise for sleeping.

PJ, my seven-year-old grandson, outfitted with a glass jar and small net from their home fish tank, chased pollywogs around like a man on the hunt for wild game. Splashes and grunts of frustration mixed with success permeated the air. This accelerated and grew in volume as he moved to bigger exploits of minnows and crawdads. Our first and only grandson, we reveled in his manliness. Esther adored this spunky boy, her only nephew. Our granddaughter, Cassidy, being a local, swung in and out of camp with her teen friends. They set up chairs in the middle of the shallow creek and between water wars helped PJ in his quest for creek critters.

The girls and I took turns paddling our air mattresses upstream and allowed the gentle current to carry us back to camp. One time as we re-entered our campsite, a great commotion of girly squeals, male shouts, and flailing bodies fled the area near a fallen log. A snake nest had been discovered with oodles of baby water moccasins. Where there were babies there might be a mama and papa —so much for our relaxed easy pace. Of course, we were reassured when the guys told us the snakes were more afraid of us than we were of them. "Yeah, right. Not!"

Esther, born with a love of the great outdoors, embraced these canvas shelters. A little tent fabric seemed spun into her DNA. Much to her chagrin, by the time she was two years old, my thirty years of camping put me into the category of : *been there, done that, over it.* Our worn-out pop-up camper reflected my personal stance. So, she seized outdoor snoozing when and where ever she could. Swaying in a cozy hammock felt like a bit of paradise.

We often met the nicest people at campgrounds. The couple next to us were not only friendly, but good at fly fishing and had all the gear. If you're as ignorant about fishing as I am, fly fishing is not using flies as bait. Our gracious neighbors lent us their equipment and taught us how. Seth a usual participant in more active sports seemed to enjoy this laid-back recreation along with PJ.

The park closed its gates at 10 p.m. so Seth and I left the campsite to drive back to Jayne's air-conditioned homestead and sleep in a real bed. *My* kind of camping.

After a good night's sleep, we returned the next morning. Our olfactory senses heightened as the salty aroma of bacon sizzling over an open fire caused our tummies to flip and gurgle. We loved this best-of-both-worlds camping experience. My heart filled with all the things which mattered: focused family time, campfires, nature, fresh air, board games, comfy sleeping quarters, and meals over a firepit.

Jayne, not in the best mood, related her lack of sleep due to an early visitor. At dawn, a black-crow-alarm grated out his harsh song in the tree above their tent. Ahh, the joys of the great outdoors. If Jayne had a gun, we might have noticed scents of singed crow amidst the bacon's fragrance by the next morning. Each day brought a new story of the crow's return and all the antics of trying to shoo it away: quiet hissing, arm waving, squirt guns, and throwing frisbees. Screaming wasn't an option as most campers snoozed away, oblivious to their pesky visitor.

A new day found us discovering ways to entertain ourselves without electronics as I created French braids for Esther and Jayne.

Playing in the creek once again, we realized the flat rocks were perfect for skipping and a contest began. It didn't take long for the Rock Skipper King to rise to the top. My husband, Seth, is a natural athlete and anything related to sports is easy for him. We quickly stopped competing and started counting. By the time he hit ten, we were all clapping, cheering, and hooting like a bunch of rednecks—northern-style of course. Esther filmed the event of his award winning thirteen bounces.

That evening we played board games under eerie flying-saucer-shaped lights. A special Jayne-touch. She'd worked hard to add her special love-pats to our vacation. A clear evening sky found us winding down by the fire pit. Later, we all climbed in our cars and headed to a big open field by the campground entrance.

Lightning bugs were out in all their flickering glory. We rolled out blankets and sleeping bags and with noses turned toward the black velvet sky, our breath caught short as we viewed the heavens uninhibited by city lights. "Wow! Amazing!" Waterfalls of exclamations poured out.

The stars did their twinkling dances and occasionally one would plummet toward earth accompanied by our vocal sighs of delight.

After a few minutes, a lone steady bright light appeared and hovered for a while. As we began to point and express our wonder at what it could be—it suddenly went dark. UFO, I'm sure. At the very least it made our hearts beat a little faster and added an aura of mystery to the night.

At the time, our family didn't realize what a gift Jayne gave us July 4, 2009. It would be the best trip our family ever experienced and become more precious in the future.

When we returned home, Esther sent a heartfelt thank you note to Jayne.

Based on their names, Esther addressed Jayne as Lady Jane and Jayne referred to Esther as Lady Liz. Perhaps the result of too much Downton Abbey?

July 1-4, 20014

Dear Lady Jayne,

I had so much fun "chillin" with you at Abrams' Creek last weekend. Thank you for all your hard work, planning and setting everything up...it was __the best__ camping trip ever!

Floating down the creek among the towering ancient trees, tadpole hunting, fly fishing, rock collecting, games under the alien lights, swinging cares away in the hammock, a symphony of fireflies in the field, star gazing, meteor shower, and the UFO! Winding down by the flickering campfire, making new friends, waking up at the "crow" of dawn, savoring the taste of campfire bacon and eggs, spending "down-to-earth" time with family, rock skipping contest and Daddy the champion with 13 skips! These are the memories I will treasure forever!

I love you and appreciate you my dear sister.

Lady Liz

REFLECT

Are you bored with superficial relationships? Tired of technology's depersonalizing your interactions with others? Do you long for meaningful times of laughter and sharing your heart with family and friends face to face? Would you even know where to begin to achieve that?

(I wrote this long before the Coronavirus hit, so as I see the results of "Sheltering in Place" on Facebook, there's been some great family time given to us. Don't waste it.)

APPLY

The purpose of sharing our family's camping story is to highlight the importance and healing power of face-to-face relationships without empty distractions and fake connections.

According to an article by Victoria Dunckley M.D. in *Psychology Today* magazine, "Neuroimaging research shows excessive screen time damages the brain." Not just addicted gamers, but the average child's seven hours of daily computer interaction.

Combining such isolation with grief sets up a formula for deep depression and a block to the healing so desperately needed.

The Center for Disease Control (CDC) reports the leading cause of death in youth ages 10 to 19, is suicide. The lack of personal connection and meaningful conversations is literally killing us.

You don't need a camping trip to turn off electronic devices and create opportunities for one on one conversations.

- Simple board game nights, a hike and a picnic, or a time of improv jiving to your favorite tunes creates a wonderful atmosphere of fun interaction and relationship building.
- Use your internet search engines for ideas to fit your family's interests.
- Take on a family project of community outreach.
- Your family is worth fighting for!

PRAYER

Dear Heavenly Father, building family connections is challenging, but maybe this time of grief is a springboard to help me bond deeper with friends and loved ones; a reminder my tomorrows are not guaranteed. Heal me Father, mend my broken heart. Above all, may my faith and trust in you become unshakeable.

Chapter 17
White Owl

When the night comes,

and you don't know which way to go

Through the shadowlands,

and forgotten paths,

you will find a road.

Lyrics by Josh Garrels

Esther's Journal

I want to fly out and see Kay and thank her for planting the seed of spiritual warfare singing and worship in me. So powerful!

Kay was the mother of Megan, Esther's childhood friend. Kay loved on Esther and mothered her in many ways. This warfare singing was passed onto me also as I experienced the inexplicable comforting power brought to Esther and myself on many pain-filled nights. I'd wondered how Esther learned to sing through her pain.

I'm forever grateful to Kay. Our lives are a tapestry and each friend's thread significant.

Music was a major theme throughout Esther's life. She played piano and flute and loved to sing. She listened to melodies spanning genres of the great classical masterpieces to the Beatles, and Christian worship music. The origin and powerful use of worship songs eased her through great suffering.

Esther discovered a new music artist-singer-lyricist, named Josh Garrels.

The White Owl song gripped me, spoke over me and I loved it—the lyrics and the music.

Its haunting melody dripped with mystery and depth which seemed foretelling to her.

White Owl

"Like a wolf at midnight howls,

you use your voice in darkest hours.

To break the silence and power,

holding back the others from their glory.

Every story will be written soon.

The blood is on the moon.

Morning will come soon.

Child the time has come for you to go

You will never be alone

Every dream that you have been shown

Will be like a living stone

Building you into a home

A shelter from the storm. "

(Lyrics used with permission by Josh Garrels)

And you are living stones that God is building into his spiritual temple. What's more, you are his holy priests. Through the mediation of Jesus Christ, you offer spiritual sacrifices that please God.

I Peter 2:5 NLT

She underlined these words…

"*Child, the time has come for you to go, and, every dream that you have been shown will be like living stone.*"

The next day's journal entry references the words: "It's time for you to go,"—she is puzzled at their meaning.

I don't understand the context, I don't want to leave Dark 2 Light Ministries. Do you mean leave the city? I don't get it, please show me.

To me, these lyrics which stood out to her, were predictive. Deep calls to deep, your days are short and time is close for you to come to your eternal home.

REFLECT

Worship songs bring us into God's presence in a special way. This truth will be demonstrated more fully in Chapter 28, Songs in the Night.

Consider the book of Revelation in the Bible... it is hymn laden with more hymns than any other book in the New Testament. All the major events of the book are accompanied by heavenly hymns. (Google Songs of the Seer: The Purpose of Revelation's Hymns by Robert S. Smith)

APPLY

One of the most difficult things is to remember and *choose* to sing or speak worship to God in the middle of your heartache. Do it anyway! Make it a habit. Prepare by having hymn and praise music lyrics printed and close by: Next to your bed, your favorites taped to the mirror in your bathroom, or in your car. Make a file on your phone or electronic devices. If you have voice assistants like Alexa or Siri use them.

PRAYER

Dear Heavenly Father, thank you for not giving up on me when I sometimes wallow in my grief and sadness when you've provided everything I need for healing and joy through your Son, Jesus. I choose to use the tools of joy you've provided through song.

Chapter 18

Spirals

From hurricanes to galaxies, seashells to flowers, the spiral is encoded into the world around us and has a universal appeal. It resonates with the human spirit. Spirals are complex yet simple, intriguing and beautiful. Such was the lure to Esther of this art form—but as in art, spirals of life can ascend or descend.

Esther's work at Dark 2 Light became a safe haven for her but financial contentions at home spun out of control.

As Esther entered the year of 2015, Romeo's verbal rages became more frequent. Money spent during Christmas at Disney on relatives visiting from overseas sent his online business into a tailspin. Esther *begged* him not to take on such unaffordable debt. Treating his guests to Disney's Magic Kingdom destroyed their budget once again.

Risking her own health—visions of their own home propelled Esther to slog through many early morning hours on a sizable freelance design project in addition to her full-time position at Dark 2 Light.

I can imagine the intense disbelief in her tear-rimmed eyes as Romeos demanded these hard-earned funds which they'd mutually agreed would go into savings. Exhaustion plus the sting of betrayal once again cut deep. Seth and I knew well the drama of Romeo's financial irresponsibility.

One evening mid-January, Esther's voice, animated and happy, called to share the news. "Marmie, guess what? A professional counselor has donated her time to the staff of Dark 2 Light! I'm working on getting an appointment for Romeo and me. If he won't go, I'll go alone."

Overjoyed, Esther scheduled an appointment.

Romeo went.

Nothing changed.

His verbal abuse *increased.*

The first weekend in February, Romeo's screaming rage suddenly morphed into a gentleness that belied his former cruelty. As Esther left for work the next morning, he told her his online business had been shut down. Her heart plummeted.

As I read about Romeo's verbal assaults in Esther's journal, I found the obvious signs of manipulation alarming; a man absorbed with his own welfare and control at any price.

A fragile butterfly tangled in a spider's netting, Esther seemed caught in a web of an abused wife and an innocent victim of Stockholm Syndrome. This is where an emotional attachment to an abuser is formed as a result of continuous stress, dependence, and a need to cooperate for survival.

That may seem an extreme statement, but as a Christian believing in the sanctity of marriage, divorce was not an easy option. She felt locked in a cage—even if she had naively crawled in on her own.

Most of Esther's friends, if not all, were unaware of what she lived with, so their consistent advice of, "you should obey your husband," stifled her own voice.

In her book, "The Rock, the Road and the Rabbi," Kathie Lee Gifford, an avid student of the Bible says, "When people speak into another's life, it's often what they've been told by others and not what the Bible actually says." She uses Ephesians 5:22 as an example. Paul exhorts, *wives, submit yourselves to your own husbands as you do to the Lord.* The Greek word for submit is *hupatasso*, which means *to identify* with or *be in support of.* This is different from the English translation taken from the Greek word, hupeiko, meaning to *submit to.* The biblical meaning of submission in Ephesians 5, has nothing to do with being a doormat or second-class citizen. Instead, it seems to point to what Jesus taught: be kind, love one another, be of service to one another and treat others the way you want to be treated. Ephesians 5 continues, we are to submit to *each other* in the fear of God. A husband is to love his wife as he loves his own body and as Christ loved the church and sacrificed himself for her.

If the cost of saving a marriage is destroying a woman, the cost is too high. God loves people more than He loves institutions.

"Cherished" by Gary Thomas

Valentine's Day

Bleeding hearts a perfect symbol of our Valentine's day

February 2015

Who would've thought I'd have such a terrible Valentine's Day? I really wasn't expecting much in the first place, but I was expecting to go home. I felt like I'd been bullied, pushed, and kicked around until I gave in. I didn't know how to change it or make it stop, but then, I realized—I had a choice. So, I took it and didn't go home. Now, I've defined the places where I stand, and to stand on them gives me strength. My heart was ripped apart that 14th night. In my devotional, I read, 'Today things may become completely calm.' This battle has been intense and fierce, I long for this calm to rest in.

Standing up for myself has been incredibly tough. I have chosen how I will live and I will not be moved.

Esther's prayer... I am stunningly light, but you are incredibly strong, you are my rock and my salvation: you are my defense, I shall not be moved.

1. *I will live in my own home without fear.*
2. *I will not be a verbal punching bag.*
3. *I will not take the blame for your actions.*
4. *I will not be bullied around.*
5. *I am worth it.*

This Momma's heart shouted, "Amen!"

My natural bent of mercy, still caused my mind to resist the possibility Romeo could be so heartless and cold to Esther's needs and sensitive heart. Even the needs of her physical body were still so compromised from the effects of cancer and the extensive chemo and radiation. I can't wrap my mind around anyone being so cruel and manipulative to this beautiful soul.

I make excuses for him, even shift the blame to myself. Over the last few years, I've *chosen* to forgive him. I still pray for his healing and for God's love to become a living breathing reality in his life—Esther desired the same.

REFLECT

Are you consistently dishonored in a relationship? Are you experiencing abuse in your marriage? As a man? As a woman? Physically? Emotionally? How do you handle gross disrespect or being told you have to put up with this?

APPLY

Read Ephesians 5 in two or three translations or the paraphrase of The Message.

I highly recommend two resources:
* The book, "Cherish" by Gary Thomas.
* YouTube video series of Love, Dates and Heartbreaks by Andy Stanley.

PRAYER

Dear Heavenly Father, you know my relationships and my heart. Guide me through Your Word, to seek out people and resources to gain a heart of wisdom and attain balanced relationships of love and personal safety.

Chapter 19

Camping in the Snow

Rain dripped from our umbrellas as bone-chilling air seemed bent on dampening our spirits and trip. Then we discovered the Smokey Mountain River Trail. Bundled up, we defied the elements as we set off for a hike. The raw dampness, drizzling rain and gurgling river brought an excitement of adventure into the unique barren surroundings. We became playful children splashing through puddles under a forest of leafless trees. An empty path usually canopied with green and lined with wild flowers and hikers, left us free to fill it with our own laughter and joy.

At 10 p.m. the previous evening I'd received a call from Esther...

"Marmie, how would you and Dad like to go on a road trip with me? Romeo and I were supposed to leave tonight but he can't go. I have time off and don't want to miss it or lose our time share points. We booked three nights in Gatlinburg, Tennessee and four in Gordonsville,

Virginia. I know this is last minute, but would you please go with me?"

Seth and I both had full work schedules. I don't like sudden changes, plus, self-employed meant no work, no pay. To go meant we needed to be packed and ready to leave the next morning. Yikes! I hung up and discussed it with Seth. The trip, a definite "Yes!" It didn't take long to switch gears and realize what a gift we'd be given— quality time with our dear girl.

Esther, although not a tom-boy, became fascinated with trees at an early age. Many pictures were the result as she posed beside these wooden props. On the trail, a discovery of a tree with twirling branches resulted in her comical Medusa pose.

Her picture with a gutted, tough-survivor of a tree, now seems symbolic of Esther's own coming battle to survive and her tenacious will to live. The surrounding green moss is symbolic of her life continued on another plain when her own soil became too impacted for her earthbound life to continue. The river—crystal waters flowing from God's throne.

Then the angel showed me the river of the water of life,

as clear as crystal,

flowing from the throne of God and of the Lamb.

Rev. 22:1

Although suffering approached, her *eternal* future glowed bright.

During the night, a dusting of snow, covered Gatlinburg. We sat on the chilly balcony the next morning and enjoyed the white glimmering scenery and some momma-daughter conversation.

The next day, the scent of fresh-brewed coffee tantalized our senses as we entered through the double wooden doors of the restaurant. A gift shop glutted with everything from unique clothing, knick-knacks, to candies from the 1950's. We squeezed sideways through a throng of people waiting to be seated. Our tummy grumblings were met with whiffs of promised breakfast fare, and our ears with a down-home country tune. A Cracker Barrel's welcomed embrace.

With full happy bellies we continued our road trip across the state of Virginia, dazzled by a landscape blanketed with several inches of snow.

Remember Esther's love for camping? Well, she surprised us with a new meaning of the concept as we entered the resort. Not only were we camping right in the middle of winter with a snow-covered backdrop, but it seemed we'd been transported to the Middle East. Nomad-style tents, minus the arid hot temperatures of the desert, were plopped onto frozen farmland.

If you've heard of a Yurt, an upscale tent, you'll know this canvas structure is certainly warmer, yet retains a camping aura. Whether listening to wind, rain, or sounds of the night, you experience the elements—but on a more comfortable level. A new experience for us all which provided the best of both worlds.

February 2015

I'm finally beginning to relax and rest as I lay in this round place. Yes, this yurt... this luxurious tent is growing on me. It's so unusual. It feels so safe and sturdy yet the sounds of nature are crystal clear.

For a tree lover, it can't get much better than our frolic the next day near President Jefferson's home of Monticello in nearby Charlottesville. Centuries old poplar trees, taken out by disease, created a tree-playground near this famous landmark.

A crowning touch to the end of our day? Lunch at Michie's Tavern. A famous landmark with the ambiance of an eighteenth-century inn, located a half mile below Jefferson's Monticello home.

This charming rustic restaurant rendered an experience rich in southern hospitality as servers in period attire offered up bountiful portions of mouth-watering fried chicken and generous helpings of all the appropriate side dishes.

A renewed and rested trio, we arrived home the next day with priceless memories tucked into our hearts.

James 1:17 KJV

Every good and perfect gift is from above and cometh down from the Father of lights...

REFLECT

Do you remember a time when an event or an opportunity covered with God's fingerprints, plopped into your life? Did you recognize it as a gift? Did God use it to sustain you through unforeseen future difficulties and even tragedy?

APPLY

These are the times you need to journal, as your memories, like melting ice-cubes, slip away so easily. Then take time at the end of a month, or quarter, or at years end and review. You'll be amazed and encouraged by the ways God has met you. You'll be lifted out of a pit the enemy of your soul would love to keep you trapped in. God's faithfulness will be evident.

PRAYER

Dear Heavenly Father, may I recognize and be thankful for the good things you bring into my life. It's so easy to forget all the little and big ways you've met me, directed me, and loved on me in the past. God you've said in Psalm 22 you inhabit the praises of your people. What an opportunity I have to be surrounded by the presence of your glory. I will remember and I will praise you.

Chapter 20
Prophesy of Isaiah 57

If I'd known what would be revealed to me in the next hour, I may have plugged my ears and started chanting loud, "La-la-la-la-la-la-la-la, I can't hear you." But I would have missed the peace and resource to help carry me through the onslaught of future malevolent challenges.

May 1st, two months after our week of adventures in the snow, Esther crumbled as debilitating pain started in her right side and leg. Two more long months and a plethora of medical tests and procedures confirmed Esther's cancer had returned. A new tumor wrapped around her ureter, a tube which excretes waste from the kidneys to the bladder, had compromised kidney function.

Two surgeons were required for the surgery; an oncologist to remove the cancerous tumor and a urologist to reposition the bladder and reattach the ureter. No laparoscopic surgery could be used. The thought of a massive incision into her precious body, although essential, caused my own gut to cringe. The possibility cancer had spread further than scans revealed left its muddy trail of fear. My heart ached at the thought of the pain and scarring she'd endure.

Gathered in our cozy kitchen nook the last of June 2015, a somber trio sat eating a breakfast of oatmeal and fruit with Silver Zhen White Tea. Our family had spent many hours here sharing tasty home cooked meals while spilling our hearts amidst laughter, tears, and prayers. Seth, Esther and I faced a long day of pre-op appointments and several lab tests before Ether's scheduled surgery on July 5th. If you've had surgery, you know the process of signing your life away on the dotted line.

Together we shared the reading of the day from Sarah Young's devotional, Jesus Calling. In some inconceivable way God often knew the exact words we needed.

Taste and see that the Lord is good; blessed is the man who takes refuge in him

Psalm 34:8

Esther and Seth left the kitchen to get ready while I sat alone—pondering. This time I didn't get it. I thought, *What an odd scripture for such a depressing day. Nothing tasted good about it. Nothing!* Now I realize I'd missed the point. The Lord tastes good, not the situation.

The second scripture shed light…

For my thoughts are not your thoughts,

neither are your ways my ways, declares the LORD.

As the heavens are higher than the earth,

so are my ways higher than your ways

and my thoughts than your thoughts."

Isaiah 55:8-9

While I meditated on this, my eyes drifted to a scripture on the opposite page. Three words seemed to highlight themselves and capture my attention. *The righteous perish.*

I began reading:

The righteous perish, and no one takes it to heart;

the devout are taken away, and no one understands

that the righteous are taken away to be spared from evil.

Those who walk uprightly enter into peace;

they find rest as they lie in death.

Isaiah 57:1-2

A lifelong student of the Bible, I questioned, *where did these verses even come from? I don't remember ever seeing them before.* It was then God's Spirit gave me understanding. A familiar *knowing*—God was speaking directly to me through his word and preparing me for what was to come.

During the previous two months when I considered my life without Esther, I didn't want to live. I railed and pleaded, "Please Lord, let me go to the grave with her. It's too much pain and loss. *I don't know how to watch my daughter die!*"

As odd as it sounds, when I read those two verses, my spirit calmed and understanding became clear. I thought, *if you need to take her to* **protect** *her Lord, I can live with that.*

In the past, I knew other sweet people taken from this earth early, and couldn't help but cry out, "Why, God?!" These verses in Isaiah opened up a new window for me to see God's heart, and it was a good one, full of compassion and desiring our best.

The past two months had been filled with intense arguments between Romeo and Esther as she stood firm on her decision of no more chemo or radiation. I'd already watched her go through such intense suffering, physically and emotionally, if God's goodness took her to deliver her from harm and evil, how could I say anything but, "Thy will be done."

As I entered my bathroom to finish getting ready, the revelation made full impact. A razor-sharp dagger hit the soft spot of my mother-heart. I crumpled to the floor dragging towels draped on the back of the door with me. Face buried in terry-cloth fibers, between heaving sobs, I cried out, "Lord, you're taking my girl, aren't you?" With crystal clarity, he replied to my spirit—*She's not yours, she's mine.* Just as I had *known* I was to have another baby and Esther was born; I now *knew*—this reverse birth would deliver her into Jesus' arms.

I couldn't share this revelation with her. It was not my place to steal her hope or crush her spirit. The battle with cancer would take great endurance regardless of the outcome. As future events played out, this revelation sometimes shredded my heart and other times brought great confidence and peace.

What person can wrap their mind around their death at age 31? I didn't want to believe it either, so with her, we prayed and hoped for a miraculous healing. I knew what God revealed to me, but I prayed for her physical restoration, sang worship songs and encouraged her in her faith.

Life is so precious and the will to live so powerful.

REFLECT

Has there ever been a time when a word, phrase, or verse of the Bible popped off the page and seemed highlighted just for you?

APPLY

In Hebrews 4:12, God's Word is described as *living* and *active*, so we shouldn't be surprised when it stirs our soul with a personal revelation. When we're suffering and desperate, we may be more alert to His voice. Although this wasn't a message anyone would want to hear, to have the Living God, Creator of all, soul-speak into your life is an indescribable experience. The choice is available to everyone.

Maybe you have never read a Bible. Perhaps you don't even own one. Not to worry, as your cell phone is an amazing tool to connect you to just the right passages. Just speak "Hey Google, scriptures on peace, comfort, and fear" or whatever your need is." Most everyone today carries the living Word of God in their hand or pocket.

PRAYER

Heavenly Father, I want to connect with you and know your heart and will for me through the stories, letters and psalms from your Word, the Bible. It's so exciting to know how much you want me to know you. Shake up my soul, enlighten my understanding, quench my thirst for peace through your Word in my present grief and trials.

Chapter 21

Surgery and Orchids

Intensity colored Romeo's voice as he asserted, "We need to contact your oncologist *today* and set up chemo appointments."

Esther locked eyes with Romeo and stated with galvanized clarity, "I've told you...I will *never* do chemo again!"

The afternoon of Esther's surgery found her surprisingly alert. Romeo stood beside her as I looked on from the end of her bed. Our family had agreed, this time we'd *not* offer opinions unless asked. Treatment had to be her decision. Still, the chemo wars were heating up again.

July 6, 2015

I've been putting off updating my journal because it means this is really happening again. But I know you all want to know what's going on with me and how the surgery went, so here it goes.

The surgery went well, they removed a golf-ball sized cancerous tumor and a section of my right ureter, also my ovary, and fallopian tube. The cancer was not soft tissue sarcoma as they thought leading up to the surgery. It is Squamous Cell Carcinoma of the internal organs, just like the last time. The good news, I was able to keep my right kidney, and have my right ureter plugged back into my bladder successfully. I am in pain and I feel like I have been run over by a train. I will have to stay at Saint Joseph's Hospital for five days. Right now, I am focusing on healing from the surgery. My doctor said after I heal from this, we'll discuss ongoing treatment. That is all I know for now.

In His hands,

Esther

God's tender touches were evident in every step of her journey. Esther's hospital room became inundated with an extravagant variety of orchids.

July 2015

Dear Friends and Family,

I'm sitting here with my friends, marveling at all the beautiful orchids that surround us. We looked up the meaning of the orchid flower and found that in ancient times it was said to cure disease and in the Victorian age it signified a beautiful lady. So, to me it's as though God orchestrated a shower of orchids over me the last two weeks with a special message. I've received a total of nine orchids among other flowers.

These last couple days have been painful and difficult for me but the flow of smiles, gifts and flowers have encouraged me and lifted my spirits. I don't know what's next, so I'm taking it one day at a time. Thank you for all your prayers, encouraging words, gifts, good food and good company.

Esther

It's day six at the hospital and I ate solid food for the first time in a week! Every day I am supposed to do laps around the nurse's station with my rolling I.V. stand. It helps the healing process and keeps me from getting blood clots. It's actually more of a slow shuffle, but today I broke my record and did three and a half laps!

The nurses were a little slow today in bringing my pain meds, so my pain episode lasted longer than usual, but "the patient" got some pampering. One friend massaged my feet with cocoa butter, another put beautiful braids in my hair, and my sister Jayne fed me salmon and rice for dinner.

A colorful handmade quilt is laying across me. The ladies at my Aunt Katrina's church made this, and if you look closely, you can see it's covered in little yellow knots. As each person made their knot, they said a prayer for me. So, I am literally covered in prayer.

(Dictated by Esther to her sister, Jayne.)

Esther

It's day seven and I found out tomorrow I will have my staples taken out and will be discharged from the hospital. I will be taken to my parents' house where my Mom will take care of me. My Aunt Katrina flew down from Washington D.C. to help out too.

Today I spent most of the day with my parents and my aunt. It felt good to be loved on by my family.

The last seven days have been really tough and painful, but they also had a silver lining, as I was showered with visits and flowers, balloons, cards, presents, and so much love and care. This was so humbling and helped take my mind off myself and be grateful for all of you.

Then we received a card with a check for $700.00, an "emergency refrigerator fund" from our "Through Thick and Thicker," international friends. Repairs were needed as it broke down right before my surgery. We cannot even begin to express our gratefulness.

REFLECT

When's the last time you received encouragement in the midst of conflict, fear, or emotional pain? Who or what encouraged you? Have you personally let the people involved know how grateful you were? Have you thanked God?

APPLY

Like Esther, be honest about the suffering, but look for the moments of good tucked in hidden places. Listen to the song "Blessings" by Laura Story and google the backstory.

PRAYER

Heavenly Father, I don't like the thought blessings might come through raindrops, sleepless nights and tears; yet I'm learning your ways *always* have my best interest at heart in the end.

Chapter 22

Confusion

A mixture of vexation, ill temper, and exasperation grated deep.

Seven months had passed since the onset of Esther's hip and leg pain, yet no doctor or professional pursued the reason. She endured with strong pain killers.

The next weeks were clouded with conflicting doctors' opinions. Esther made an appointment with the chemo oncologist to appease Romeo and consider her input. She'd predicted a long healthy life for Esther when she treated her first cancer and was baffled to learn the cancer had returned. She now told her: "You can't use the same chemo as before as you will have built up a resistance to it. I will consult with a surgeon friend of mine who works at the world-renowned M.D. Anderson Cancer Center in Houston, Texas."

Esther set up another appointment for the following week.

Her oncologist had a reputation for being the best in the southeast. Much later, we discovered it was for the treatment of breast cancer. We found it makes a big difference.

During the following week Esther and I brainstormed and created a file of important questions. When she and Romeo walked into her appointment the following week, her oncologist seemed unsettled and distracted as Esther began her request for information. Backing toward the door, the doctor exited with a clipped statement, "I need to make a phone call."

Astonished and wide-eyed, Esther gazed at the closed door. After a long wait, a nurse came in and requested Esther's list of questions. Appalled, Esther inquired, "Where's the doctor?"

"She's with a patient," came the lame reply.

Later Esther expressed her thoughts, "My oncologist's body language exhibited such shock and distress at the cancer's return. She had been so confident the chemo and radiation would cure me. She had said, 'Esther, you're young and you have a long life ahead of you. I tell it like it is and don't sugar-coat anything.' Yet, it was back and she had no answers for me this time. Maybe she had left to put a call into the colorectal doctor she knew at M.D. Anderson Cancer Center."

Exasperated, Esther lost all confidence in her oncologist and left. Later we found the doctor from M.D. Anderson had suggested a new chemo therapy, but Esther's insurance wouldn't cover it. She wrote a plea for financial hardship but denied coverage again.

With no explanation, her oncologist wanted to proceed with the previous chemo even though Esther's body would resist it. Romeo pushed hard for Esther to move forward with the now ineffective chemo. Unyielding. Esther shot back, "No way!"

Like sails with no wind, July left us all limp with exhaustion. I found when we'd depleted our own resources, God showed up and revealed his heart.

With much joy, Esther and Romeo received a generous gift from a friend who sacrificially gave them a weekend get-a-way to North Georgia, complete with spa treatments and massages. Esther was humbled by his generosity.

August 2015

Through all this physical daily pain and emotional soulful weariness, I was set free for many hours today. I'm sitting on our balcony (an unexpected blessing) listening to the waterfall below and looking out on the blue mountains and the green valley. So peaceful here, I

***feel worlds away. This calm before the storm is precious
to me and I will store it deep in my heart.***

© © ©

The same day, I sat at home updating my journal as a
thunderstorm rumbled and steady showers pelted the
thirsty green landscape. I sipped English Breakfast tea as
the song, "I Will Praise You in This Storm," by Casting
Crowns played in the background. Emotional exhaustion
gave way to my own cloudburst as tears cascaded. The
song—a lament mixed with a choice to believe in the
whispers of a good God regardless of my circumstances.

I was sure by now God,

You would have reached down and wiped our tears away,

Stepped in and saved the day

But once again, I say "Amen" and it's still raining.

Against all common sense, I lifted my hands to
praise the God who sometimes gives and takes away.
Every word and phrase of the song mirrored my soul—yet
once again these strains of worship helped me process my
grief and ushered me to a place of extraordinary peace.

It's one thing to sing Amazing Grace—it's quite
another to experience it.

REFLECT

Does your Emmanuel, the God who's supposed to be *with you,* seem far away? Do tears mirror pellets of stinging rain with no comfort in sight?

APPLY

Listen to "Praise You In This Storm," by Casting Crowns Worship Band on YouTube.
https://youtu.be/0YUGwUgBvTU

PRAYER

My Puzzling Heavenly Father, I choose to raise my hands of fragile faith and raspy voice of praise, even when the storm rages.

Chapter 23

Abandoned!

Marmie, Vera just left!" Esther's panicked voice cried.

"What?! What do you mean she left?"

Surely, I'd misunderstood. A close friend doesn't desert someone they genuinely care about.

I'd just arrived at my sister's home near Washington D. C. to rest and renew. One of Esther's dearest friends, Vera, had time off from work and volunteered to move in to Esther's home for two weeks and assist with her care: transport her to and from work, make fresh green drinks, create healthy meals, and keep up with other protocols. Vera, a tireless researcher, worked consistently to unearth more information on healthy choices to treat cancer. I knew Esther would be in good hands as I boarded the plane.

"Marmie, she's not coming back!"

"But why?" I probed. Vera, a loyal friend, would never just choose to leave.

"Mom, the quarrel between her and Romeo on the way home from my doctor's appointment today frightened her."

My outrage mushroomed into more questions than Esther could answer. I hung up and called Vera. I needed to hear the story from her lips.

"After Romeo's insistence, Esther saw her oncologist one more time. The three of us went to her appointment. When she and Romeo walked out of the doctor's office, they were arguing and Esther stated firmly, 'I'm *not* doing chemo!' Romeo, became furious at her refusal. After we entered the elevator, he took Esther by the shoulders and physically shook her and screamed into her face. He frightened me. I shouted at him to *stop*."

"As we left the parking lot, he ran the car into a curb barely avoiding a crash. I told him to pull over and quit acting like a crazy man. He calmed down some, but continued a tirade of objections to Esther's decision. We made it home, but his fury terrified me. He then *demanded* for me to leave. Physically shaking from the intensity of his anger, I left."

Vera continued, "I don't understand what happened. Last night I'd fixed Esther a healthy meal and she went to bed early. Romeo and I watched a video titled, *Forks Over Knives*, on alternative cancer treatments. Then we had a pleasant discussion about it and he seemed fine."

Bereft, and sick to my stomach I felt frightened for the well-being of my dear girl. The rest of the week Esther stayed at home and other friends helped where they could. Romeo cut off interaction with Seth and me, and became more hostile to our family. Vera cut off all contact with Romeo for the next seven months due to her fear of him.

© © ©

Daily, Seth and I researched cancer therapies and discovered The Cancer Treatment Centers of America who promoted alternatives along with chemo. A new center had just opened in Atlanta. After more enquiries we found the best CTCA facility for her needs would be the original location in Tulsa, Oklahoma. Her insurance covered the tests, and it seemed a good combination of both worlds.

Esther arrived at CTCA in Oklahoma for a week of testing on Sept 2, 2015. A promise from the medical team to solve the mystery of her intense hip and leg pain gave us great hope. I longed to be there, but Romeo said, "No!" We only supported Esther's desires and added none of our own thoughts unless asked. I told Esther to call me if at any point she felt I could come without bringing more conflict.

Romeo left his coaching and on-line business to go with her; but mid-week, he abruptly announced to Esther he had to go home. He made an impromptu call to Esther's friend, Heidi, in Colorado and requested she come to be with Esther in Tulsa the rest of the week. This put her into a whirlwind of activity to find care for her two young children, but this loyal friend made it happen. Getting updates regarding Esther's tests were sketchy at best. She needed an advocate there with some authority to probe until they got answers. Little did I realize Heidi's alliance with Romeo regarding chemo and believing lies about our family would become a wedge. After a tense week with little communication to us, Heidi returned home.

I love the way God encourages us in hard places and lets us know we're not alone. Mid-week, Esther remembered her childhood friend, Megan who now lived in Oklahoma. Although one-hundred miles away from Tulsa, Megan made the trek to meet Esther at CTCA.

The constant flow of tests, scans, and bloodwork became exhausting for Esther, yet by the end of the week they had no solution to the sciatic pain in her back and leg. The night before she left CTCA, a surgeon she'd never met before stopped by her room and with blunt candor delivered startling news. The horrifying report stunned her.

Her prayer journal revealed the results and her reaction.

September 2015

God, I'm mad at you! I just received some really tough news yesterday. I was told my tumor just grew back very quickly and they will need to operate and take out my right kidney, right ureter, the bladder and my uterus. I am so over this cancer thing. I contemplated what it would be like if my plane had gone down today... and it didn't seem like a bad option!

I paced and wrung restless hands as I waited for news to find out if Esther had been left to travel alone. I knew her strength was limited emotionally and physically. My anger flared white hot when I found neither Romeo or Heidi were traveling with her. Abandoned and weak, she navigated the trip. Romeo worked the evening she arrived, so her Dad and I picked her up from the airport and brought her to our home. Her wearied sadness, a palpable veil.

At the end of September, Esther visited her Atlanta cancer surgeon to go over the operative report and ask questions regarding her prior surgery from July 5th. With results from Tulsa in hand, he stated the report Esther received was wrong. The tumor had not regrown. He'd removed all the visible cancer with the section of the ureter and allowed good margins. Since he'd been the one who had internal hands on experience and actual visuals, Esther trusted him.

REFLECT

Have people disappointed you? Have you been abandoned by family and friends who should have been there for you? What do you do with that?

APPLY

"Heartache forces us to embrace God out of desperate, urgent need.
God is never closer than when your heart is aching."
Joni Eareckson Tada

Jesus suffers with us. No one knows rejection more than he. Our wanderings and bad choices may have allowed unpleasant, even terrible circumstances to crowd us to himself, the Lord of all comfort. Other times it's not personal choices, but the result of global evil that entered with Adam and Eve.

Memorize 2 Corinthians 1:3-4 NIV

Praise be to the God and Father of our Lord Jesus Christ, the Father of compassion and the God of all comfort, who comforts us in all our troubles, so that we can comfort those in any trouble with the comfort we ourselves receive from God.

PRAYER

Heavenly Father, I am totally helpless apart from you. You who have promised never to leave or forsake me. I entrust myself to your care for the uncertain days ahead.

Thank you for the promise of your saving presence and comfort.

Chapter 24

Valley of Indecision

Closing in on three months of ambivalence, our family became frantic with concern. Esther, a jelly-like mass of indecision regarding her treatment, caused us many anxious days as important healing time slipped away. A shroud of confusion seemed to cover her mind. Our family took turns going to her home the evenings Romeo coached soccer. Careful not to sway her in any direction we pleaded with her to choose a plan of action.

She continued her work at Dark 2 Light where they'd set up a recliner so she could rest when necessary. Surrounded by kindness and an atmosphere of peace, it became her haven.

Exasperated, I vented my frustration about Esther's waffling posture to my dear sister-in-law. She gave me great advice, "Get your focus off forcing a decision and plan some fun trips. Make memories with her." What an *Aha* moment. I immediately called Esther and made plans for a mother-daughter trip to North Georgia the following weekend.

© © ©

Splashes of color hinted at autumn as we left early Saturday morning. I drove, while Esther stretched out on the backseat waiting for her pain meds to kick in. Winding down hilly country roads, farms and mountain views dotted the landscape. For the exceptional vistas, I'd pull over. Esther, propped up on elbows with neck stretched long, took in the beauty and snapped an occasional picture.

We were headed for some of our favorite hangouts but also on the lookout for new ones. A backwoods route did not disappoint as we stumbled onto a quaint country café advertising *salted* coffee. Yes, you read that right, bacon, eggs, and salted coffee—what a hoot. Our giggles echoed across the countryside. Laughter felt good. To our surprise, the salted coffee even tasted good.

Esther's pain eased so we ambled through some of our favorite shops.

Most of our trips north included a visit to Mark of the Potter in Batesville, Georgia—a refurbished grist mill. We had a ritual of picking up every mug of interest to find one which conformed to our hand in shape, size and comfort. We each found a new favorite that day.

As the heart-warming day faded into dusk, Esther and I arrived at her home and enjoyed some chamomile tea in our new mugs. A pleasant evening embraced us. The sound of wood groaned as we eased ourselves down on the steps of her front porch.

Unexpectedly my thoughts went dark as a desolate sadness enveloped me. Waves of death lassoed my heart, clenching tight until I thought it would burst wide and bleed out. Fragments of Isaiah 57 revisited my mind, "The righteous perish...to be spared from evil...they find rest as they lie in death."

This cherished daughter was so much a part of me; sometimes I didn't know where I ended and she began. Yes, I realize that sounds codependent, and may have been true. We were kindred spirits, in soul and faith. Suffocating, I sat and fidgeted as I struggled long with emotions for which I had no words. Finally, I reached over and gently pulled her into my arms. Tear-drenched shoulders—the evidence of our worst fears.

☉ ☉ ☉

A mixture of joy and fear flipped my world as Esther's question flowed from my phone a week later—*Mom, would you or Dad pick me up from work today? I'm ready to start alternative treatments.*

Her decisive words, were like streams of life-giving water after a drought. I'd been waiting for definitive action for so long, my heart thumped out rhythms of a wild dance. Understanding came later when Esther explained her decision… ***While I was getting ready for work, Romeo came at me with such rage, I felt physically at risk. I grabbed my purse and went across the street to my neighbor's house and asked for a ride to work.***

I knew the incident had been serious for this patient daughter to take such quick action.

We made the long round trips from our home to Dark 2 Light throughout the rest of the week. Work was therapy for her, so we couldn't ask her to quit. We introduced a new healthy diet immediately.

She chose her treatments from the information we'd collected over the past months. A special revolutionary machine only available in Alabama drew our attention during our research. With Esther's agreement a flurry of activity resulted. We made calls to the volunteer host homes in Alabama and laid out travel plans. We left the following Saturday, October 13, 2015.

Our emotions, a complicated mix of terror, churning anxiety, and hope. We were about to cut a life and death course through uncharted waters.

REFLECT

Have you ever been so focused on a problem you overlooked the most important thing? You missed the relationship to be embraced, and a precious memory to be made? Maybe tunnel vision has held you captive?

APPLY

My tight focus on Esther's decision almost cost making a special memory with her.

Seek the counsel of trusted friends and family as you walk through mind-numbing trials. Fresh eyes and perspective are so valuable.

PRAYER

"And let us run with endurance the race God has set before us.
We do this by keeping our eyes on Jesus, the champion who initiates and perfects our faith."
Hebrews 12:1b-2a NLT

Dear Father, I realize I've been too focused on the problem. You encourage me to keep my eyes looking to you, the author and finisher of my faith. As I'm bombarded with so many emotional distractions, center my mind on what I know to be true. You are my faithful Father.

Chapter 25

God is Working While We Are Grasping

More than one person questioned, "What in the world do they have in Montgomery, Alabama you can't find in Atlanta?"

The answer, "A Photon Genius Machine which utilizes infrared electro-magnetic energy for healing. The nearest machine stood in Montgomery.

We had tried conventional medicine and since they had nothing more to offer except ineffective chemo, Esther chose nutritional supplements to fortify her immune system and the use of the Photon Genius. It offered a safe and effective therapy for cancer and other chronic illnesses without drugs or side-effects. Its history went back to the scientific genius of Nikola Tesla. (See book by Thomas Valone - Bioelectromagnetic Healing.)

Twice a day at 8 a.m. and 8 p.m. Esther used the machine for therapy.

The owner, Dot, soon became our friend. As a child in 1945, Dot had quite a story of her own using electro-magnetic therapy. She didn't know what it was called then, but when she saw the Photon Genius, she knew it had to be from the same technology which helped heal her heart condition as a child. She made the investment and bought one. It's now her business and ministry.

Esther's toes twitched when Dot put on some rhythmic music to help pass the time during her treatments. From childhood, Esther loved to dance— definitely her happy place.

One evening Dot invited her friend, David, a competitive ballroom dance instructor to Esther's session. The thought of dancing with a professional enticed her. To participate would be fun but bordered on the edge of folly because of her hip and leg pain.

Her love of dance won. With pain meds at maximum strength, her performance was not flawless but Esther followed his lead like a pro. I couldn't stop smiling as I saw her delight, but health concerns caused my heart to pound.

Dot commented, "The thing I remember about Esther's dance, was when she looked at me wreathed in smiles and said, 'Miss Dot, I don't hurt anymore!' and she whirled away. She was *so* good! Later I told her, 'Honey when you're having fun (a three-letter word for God), miracles can happen—keep dancing.' Dance is a universal language just like music; they collapse time frames and allow healing to occur."

During our first week in Alabama, we stayed with Carole Jean Boyd, a professional woodcarver. What a unique talent. We first met her as she prepared to open her new Gallery. We had connected through a contact at our church, but I'll let Esther tell this story:

We arrived Oct 16, 2015 at the first home we stayed in. It was owned by a seventy-year-old artist-woodcarver, Carole Jean Boyd. Her home was older 1970's inside and out—shag carpet and all. She made us feel so relaxed and at home. It's a beautiful story how I ended up there.

Carole Jean's daughter who was connected to my parent's church in Georgia, called her mom in Alabama —knowing her mom would never agree to volunteer— but asked if anyone at her church would be willing to host a cancer patient. To her daughter's disbelief, Carole Jean said, "Yes! I want to do it."

Carole had cancer in the past and found it painful to have any memory of it or deal with other's going through it. She had been a widow for over twenty-five years and rarely allowed any one into her home, much less complete strangers. Through a Bible Study, God had been teaching her to say, "Yes," to God's promptings. She realized she had been saying "No," for most of her life and had lost so much.

During our stay at Carole's, she opened up about her grandson who'd lived with her for a brief time. He'd become addicted to drugs and she had no idea how to help him. So, I told her I worked at Dark 2 Light. We shared deeply and laughed and cried together at how God works in the most amazing ways!

Carole Jean had her whole church praying for me, even before we arrived. Her Bible study teacher, Lesa, the one who led her to listen to God's promptings, was at the Sunday picnic we all went to. It was an honor to meet Lesa as well as the pastor and his wife.

Lesa gathered some donations from other church members and bought groceries for Jean as she was running very low on money and had an empty refrigerator. Talk about stepping out in faith! It was so special to be a part of all this.

Esther continued...

October was a tough month. I was in Montgomery, Alabama for half of it doing Photon Genius treatments to fight my cancer. During this time, I had to miss Romeo's birthday and our eight-year anniversary. Missing each one was heart-breaking and I didn't know if I could keep the course.

I called him on his birthday to ask if he would drive over. He ended up ranting and yelling that I was killing myself by not doing the chemo treatment my oncologist prescribed. (The one she said wouldn't be effective because my body had built up a resistance to it last time.) Then I realized, even on his birthday I must stand my ground. There is no excuse for someone to endure such a verbal beating, even if it's the other's birthday. So, I spent my days and nights with Dot and the Photon Genius machine and the daytime resting outside and enjoying the park or in bed at our host home.

The route of alternative healing is not for the faint of heart. The patient needs to be one-hundred percent in sync with the caregivers, involved in the research, keep a positive mindset, and willing to do whatever it takes to beat the beast.

REFLECT

The title of this book is Grief is Not my *Future*, but where is God in the *Now*? As we grappled with life and death decisions, could it be God worked in people's lives in another dimension, a spiritual one? Maybe while we grasped at any modality to beat the cancer, God worked behind the scenes building people up on an eternal level?

APPLY

Looking through the eyes of the eternal…God saw lives being impacted for His kingdom. Not only in our family but in Carole's life. A challenge to say "Yes," and open her home and heart. A circumstance for her faith to grow when she had an empty refrigerator and watched the Lord provide. Church members were blessed as they stepped up and provided this physical need as well prayer support for Esther. Through Esther's work with Dark 2 Light, Carole received a new perspective to minister to her grandson which in turn blessed Esther. Giving sacrificially blesses the giver and joy grows. Dot gave Esther delight through music, dance, and her buoyant spirit.

Look for those gifts in your own journey. Read Roman's chapter 8. Give special focus to
Romans 8:18 NIV.

I consider that our present sufferings are not worth comparing with the glory that will be revealed in us.

PRAYER

Dear Heavenly Father, I'm beginning to see how limited my view is. I get so earth-focused on my problems big and small and lose sight of your eternal purpose. Help me to keep *your* perspective. I may experience grief...

But, it's *not my future.*

Chapter 26

Alternatives Validated

There's one clamoring question when you launch your own alternative therapy protocols... "Is what I'm doing working?"

We found three definitive tests to help determine just that. Nitric Oxide Test Strips, pH test strips, and an HCG urine test. After only four treatments in the Photon Genius, Esther's Nitric Oxide levels rose from a *depleted* range to *above normal*. We were excited. The beginning pH test was 5.0, very acidic. Cancer cells love an acidic system and can't survive in an alkaline environment. By the first of November, her pH had risen to 7.5, a perfect balance. An HCG urine test kit had to be ordered from another country. More accurate than a blood test, it reveals any abnormal division of cells in the body. If you test 50 or above, one of three things are occurring. You have a large wound healing, you are pregnant, or you have cancer.

Esther's baseline test was 53.5. Six weeks later it had lowered to 52.6 a significant drop. We were doing something right.

After returning from Montgomery, we purchased the more affordable Photon Genie, added an infrared dome to her protocols, plus multiple supplements and fresh vegetable drinks. Daily—seven days a week her regimen started at 6:30 a.m. and finished at 10 p.m. Sprinkled throughout were trips to doctors in Atlanta and Alpharetta for meds and tests, plus a Chinese acupuncturist, and our family Chiropractor.

◎ ◎ ◎

A knock at the door signaled Esther's nurse friend, Oliesa, had arrived. She noticed Esther's bloodwork report laying on the coffee table. She picked it up and exclaimed, "Oh my, I'm so surprised. I didn't expect your numbers to be so good!" Another affirmation.

Her primary care physician ordered an MRI, determined to find the reason for Esther's hip and leg pain. It revealed a herniated disc in her lower back. Dr. Mazon, our family chiropractor, began deep tissue adjustments on Esther to heal the lumbar area. He'd brought healing to our family so many times, we dubbed him Dr. Amazing.

Esther experienced reduced leg and back pain toward the end of October, so Dr. Mazon compared a new MRI with the first one. The bulging disc had shrunk in size. She'd also gained four pounds. We were on a good course.

REFLECT

Isn't it wonderful when you've put in the research the study and worked hard to solve a problem and are then validated with positive results?

APPLY

Whatever the situation...a failing marriage, a rebellious teen, or a critical medical problem, start with prayer. The beginning of knowledge is the fear of God, (simply taking God seriously). He loves you and wants the best for you. You can't control other people or the outcome but do the research so you can make good choices. With the technology available today and utilizing trained professionals as resources you can arm yourself and make wise decisions.

PRAYER

Dear Heavenly Father,

I get so emotional when surrounded by trouble. Father, help me to practice going to you with everything so it becomes a habit. You are my helper and my rock in the messiness of life.

Chapter 27

Songs in the Night

Esther and I laid in peaceful stillness as our prayers and worship songs faded. I felt God's presence wrap us in His arms like a comforting blanket, light and airy yet powerful in its weight of sweetness. Once again, the experience calmed my fractured heart and kept it from shattering. Back home after our two-week stay in Alabama, this became a typical night during her five-month stay in our home.

Esther stayed in our master bedroom on the main floor. I slept beside her attending her needs. Even though on strong pain medications, she'd awaken during the night, reach for me and with a gentle nudge request…

Marmie, it hurts so much, please sing— please pray.

I kept song sheets by the bed to aid my fuzzy, sleep-deprived brain. With a voice raw and gravely from exhaustion, I'd croak out a worship song, a prayer, or both. A palpable peaceful presence would surround us and Esther would fall back to sleep. The contradiction of God's tender nearness amidst the intense pain was baffling yet powerful.

Through the blur of frequent interrupted nights and long days, this became a regular event. When Esther could, we'd sing together. One night she quieted and fell asleep with her back to me. I heard a melody but I didn't recognize it. Puzzled, I touched her shoulder and asked, "Are you humming?" Drowsy with sleep, she replied, "No Marmie," and slipped back into tranquil slumber.

Over the next few nights, the humming performance repeated. Each time, Esther sleepily murmured, "It's not me, I don't hear anything."

Hmm, I thought, *it's coming from Esther's side of the bed, over her, not me. I could hear it, but Esther couldn't —how odd.*

I wondered, *was it coming from the fan? The heating vents? The electronic photon genie she was connected to?* I'd rouse myself and walk around to Esther's side of the bed searching for a logical reason. I switched off all machines but the humming continued.

I pondered over this for the next few nights. One evening before drifting off to sleep, I asked, "Lord, am I going crazy? Why am I hearing this? Where is it coming from?"

The next morning as I awoke, remnants of a scripture came to mind. Just the words, "He sings over you." I checked it out and was astounded as I read...

The LORD your God is with you,

he is mighty to save.

He will take great delight in you,

he will quiet you with his love,

he will rejoice over you with singing.

Zephaniah 3:17

Could this night music I heard possibly be from heaven?

Personally, I think faith expressed by prayers and worship songs in the middle of such suffering, opened a pinhole of sound from heaven. I think King David would agree.

By day the LORD directs his love,

at night his song is with me.

Psalms 42:8 NIV

I also remembered the story of the apostle Paul and Silas in Acts 16 where they prayed and sang praises in jail after a severe beating for sharing the Gospel. It caused an earthquake and opened prison doors which led to the salvation of many.

Our faith, especially in the midst of suffering is very precious to God. Oh, how he must love it when his children trust him.

He knew. He cared. He delighted in us. He sang over us. How can such joy and agony dance together?

I believe I audibly experienced the living presence of God himself—confirming his love. He *knew* and was *with us* in all we were going through. He utilized a lifetime of planting his Word in our minds to say—you *can* trust me. Evil is from the destroyer, but in the middle of the trial, you can experience my presence and be transformed.

God's perspective is eternal, beyond our personal limited knowledge or existence. If he allows this much suffering into our lives, the eternal glory will be exquisite.

It's a belief.

It's a choice.

The just shall walk by faith.

We were anchored in the Lord through his word, his songs in the night, and his beautiful presence.

REFLECT

How has God met *you* in your moments of pain or grief?

APPLY

We don't like it, but I think the hard places of suffering and desperation provide conducive conditions to sensitize us to God's voice. Also, we forget to simply *ask*. Since our lives clamor loud, we then need to be still with intentional expectation to hear the small quiet voice of His Spirit.

PRAYER

Heavenly Father, I cry to You who knows my heart and needs within my season of grief, pain, or illness. I see in Esther's story, your tender nearness. In my suffering, I desire to be enveloped in the presence of such loving kindness. Direct my steps and help me to keep the eyes of my spirit on You. Heal my heart, my soul, my body.

Chapter 28

Betrayal

Exciting news! A fun event for Esther emerged on the horizon. Her friend Heidi invited her to spend a long weekend with her at her parents' home. Esther looked forward to a fun break for her and us. The timing seemed perfect. She had just regained her strength and appetite with the help of a steroid which had given her relief from her pain. On an upswing of joy, she left for her visit.

Though Esther enjoyed the much-needed distraction with her friend, when she returned the following Tuesday, frail, and fragile as a flower petal, jokingly I scolded her for playing too hard. The rest of the week found Seth and I exhausted as we labored to stabilize her so she could eat and get relief from her new bout of pain. Our constant objective—to remove stress and rebuild her immune system so she could win this battle.

Anger mixed with shock and betrayal exploded in me much later when I found her weekend with Heidi included an invitation for Romeo to be there too. What?!

Seth and I put every ounce of strength, heart, and mind into her care, twenty-four-seven, with her agreement *not* to be in contact with Romeo at all. (Repeated incidents in the past revealed the costly emotional and physical side-effects.)

No wonder Esther came back home so compromised. The pummeling she may have withstood from Romeo, Heidi and her family would have been enough to make a well-person wilt. The conflict of conscience in Esther would have added another thick layer of stress because of her agreement with us to have no contact with Romeo. We had told her if she wanted to be with Romeo, we'd support her, but we couldn't do the 24/7 alternatives at our home and deal with his contention and anger. It undermined all our efforts. To save her life first and work on the marriage later seemed the path of wisdom.

The betrayal cut deep. I don't know if Esther knew Romeo would be there, but I know once in his presence she would have had a hard time sending him away. She couldn't afford the added conflict to her limited strength. Although, not blind to her betrayal of our trust, by the time we found out, Esther's further decline made it pointless to say anything.

What a mess from every angle. It seemed Esther tried to stay afloat the best she could in whatever sea of conflict she stumbled into.

REFLECT

Have you found yourself in a situation where you *knew* you had the right advice for a loved one or friend? Were you so arrogant you didn't hear both sides of the story? Or maybe like Esther, did you find yourself in a compromised situation too conflicted to know how to respond, or even see the betrayal your action perpetrated?

APPLY

The most hurtful thing about betrayal is that it never comes from your enemies. Betrayal by a friend or family member is one of the worst feelings ever. If you're placed in the middle of conflicting parties you love, the emotional pain is worse than a physical wound. The question is: "how do you handle betrayal?"

Only God through Christ can calm the painful storm inside us. Be still! Pour out your heart to him. You can count on God to use all the difficult things you face to be used for your good and His greater purpose. Other than Jesus, I don't know if there's a greater story of betrayal than the story of Joseph who said to his brothers, "you meant evil against me, but God meant it for good."

Forgiveness and thankfulness, that's how you handle betrayal. Forgiveness prevents it from destroying your heart. Thankfulness acknowledges God's omnipotence within the battle. Be patient with yourself as it's a process.

PRAYER

Dear Heavenly Father, I desire a peaceful loving heart, but betrayal is so painful and hard to lay down. My flesh wants validation, vengeance, or at least an apology. Your example is so opposite of mine, Lord. From a cross of the cruelest suffering you said, "Forgive them, for they know not what they do." I choose to forgive. May your Spirit help me love my enemies and remove all bitterness and anger.

Chapter 29

More Grief, More Grace

If I ever had a question about a person having a soul separate from their physical body, I had no doubt as I drifted in the twilight of wakefulness at 4 a.m. on a late autumn morning. I knew my body still laid on the bed, but a presence hovered over the floor next to me and sang an old hymn. The voice was mine although I wasn't physically singing.

Esther lay awake beside me so I told her what had happened, then googled the lyrics, and sang the revitalizing words of poetess and lyricist, Annie Johnson Flint. (1866-1932)

Annie's songs were about viewing everything in life from an eternal perspective.

He giveth more grace as our burdens grow greater,

He sendeth more strength as our labors increase;

To added afflictions, He addeth His mercy,

To multiplied trials, His multiplied peace.

When we have exhausted our store of endurance,
When our strength has failed ere the day is half done,
When we reach the end of our hoarded resources,
Our Father's full giving is only begun.

His love has no limit, His grace has no measure,
His power no boundary known unto men;
For out of His infinite riches in Jesus,
He giveth, and giveth, and giveth again.

☺ ☺ ☺

When I think back on this profound moment, I'm awed by God's fathomless personal love for me. Perfectly timed, custom-made, Esther and I were emboldened and strengthened to stand in truth and walk forward cloaked in God's peace. Hallelujah! All Glory to you, Father!

During our online research we found a new oncologist in the Atlanta area who worked with patients using alternative methods. After examining Esther, he said her pain had to be more than a herniated disc. He ordered an MRI with contrast dye and explained he'd seen another patient with similar symptoms. He felt sure he knew what caused her intense leg pain. At long last, maybe someone had an answer. We were encouraged.

He sent Esther to a new radiologist, his colleague and friend, and explained to him how to position the machine to get pictures of the area he needed to see.

A week later we received the results of the MRI. A new tumor 5 to 6 cm. (2 to 3 inches) in size had grown into her sacral plexus. (A web-like network of nerves which provides motor and sensory ability for the pelvis, thigh, lower leg, and foot.) Fingers of the tumor had grown into these nerves which made it inoperable. At last, an explanation for the intense pain she'd experienced for the last seven months. The herniated disk—a side effect.

Our family's morale plummeted into a chasm of sadness.

After Esther's massive radiation treatments in 2011, the radiologist said she maxed out her quota of radiation and should never have it again. (We didn't know this until *much* later or we would never had followed the next protocol.) The new radiologist, explained he had new state-of-the-art, high-tech equipment that would only radiate the tumor, causing little to no harm to other tissues. He predicted the tumor would shrink up to 90%. With surgery not an option, Esther chose to try his recommended twenty-eight new radiation treatments.

Entrenched in a tearful week, Esther faced a place she never wanted to go again. Just the fitting and creating of the claustrophobic body cast she'd wear for radiation treatments crushed her soul as it foreshadowed the twenty-eight times she would spend in the cold armor-padded-room—*alone*.

The harrowing reality settled in as our family gathered for dinner the night before her treatments began. We had a time of cleansing tears together. Her sister Jayne stepped forward with her ability to give an affirming big picture. She formulated a plan of positive attitudes with practical steps forward. Her good insights and uplifting words moved us to a new mindset of wholeness and hope.

After her first radiation treatment mid-December 2015, Esther languished as her body, a wet piece of tissue paper, draped our couch. Shocked by her body's reaction of extreme fatigue, she whimpered, "Oh Marmie, I never expected to feel this horrible on my *first* treatment. It wasn't like this last time."

From this point she started a steady downward spiral.

January began with Seth and I fighting off flu symptoms, vertigo, and back issues as we spent sixteen-hour days and restless nights caring for Esther. Life became a blur.

Seth slept in the guest bedroom upstairs. Mid-January as he rolled out of bed, he landed on the floor—face planted into the rug. Extreme nausea and dizziness overcame him. Downstairs where I slumbered near Esther, I experienced my own dizzy spell. My blood pressure had been high at the doctor's office the day before. Seth called for help from his cell phone. I crawled on hands and knees up the stairs with the blood pressure cuff. We both checked out in normal range. Later that day, a deep tissue massage and adjustment from our chiropractor Dr. Mazon, soon up-righted our bodies.

Trying to find the humor in our crazy out-of-control life, I wrote an e-mail at the end of the day...

The bottom line of our story is—we feel like a couple of drunken sailors trying to steer a straight course through uncharted waters. Now doesn't that just make you want to climb into our boat?

Poor Esther...lol

REFLECT

One challenge and heartache after another—how do you endure? What kind of foundation do you lay to survive such grief? What significance did this song have which entered my world in such a unique manner? What's the story behind it?

APPLY

Maybe the lyrics from Annie's song resonate with your present world of burdens, labors, afflictions, trials, exhaustion, failed strength, and no resources. If you know the song, sing it. If not, find it on YouTube. Learn it. Sing it as a prayer. Claim the resources as your own by faith.

God's provisions are available, but sometimes it takes hitting the wall and crumpling to the floor to experience them. It's then we open our hands to receive God's gifts of more grace and strength, more mercy, more peace, limitless love, measureless grace, power, and infinite riches.

Check out the backstory of Annie Johnson Flint's life. What happened that allowed her to write such soul-stirring lyrics? Great enduring songs usually come with a story.

http://www.homecomingmagazine.com/article/he-giveth-more-grace/

PRAYER

Dear Heavenly Father,

I thank you for your limitless love, for your patience with me when I'm slow, thick-headed or willful. The joy of your grace is always more than abundant to exceed my grief.

Chapter 30

I Believe!

At 1:00 a.m. odd snickering sounds came from Esther's side of the bed. *That* was a first. Concerned I asked, "What's wrong?" With a strong voice, she announced, "I have no pain!" I couldn't believe lack of pain woke her up in the middle of the night. Crazy! The doctor had started her on a nerve pain blocker and it worked. Soon, pure joy erupted as our duet of chuckles resonated in the dark. The rest of the night I woke occasionally to the soft wafting sounds of her giggles.

January 2016, I read through my e-mails of the previous four months and realized I sounded so positive and strong. The strength came through a veil of intense suffering as I cried out, "Help me, God!" Anything but a superstar Christian, I desired for people to know the source of my strength, so I shared more honestly...

Day to day, in-the-moment reality, I cry, have a hurting heart beyond description. I fall on my face in fear and doubt. Today I'm mentally and emotionally on the floor and need lifting up to our faithful God! Seth does too. I know when people are praying. I'll look back over a day and exclaim, 'Wow, we made it through some insane events, but my heart is peaceful and full of hope.'

January 27, 2016, Esther had her twenty-eighth and final radiation treatment. She would have to wait three weeks to let the radiation finish working before having an MRI to see how much the tumor had shrunk. From the time Esther started radiation mid-December 2015, it had been difficult to keep her on all the healthy protocols. She lost her appetite and with it seven pounds. Her color faded to pale parchment and extreme weakness set in along with many complications.

Our hope-filled faces turned toward the oncologist as he entered the room to reveal the MRI results. Esther's anxious questioning eyes met mine. How much had the tumor shrunk after twenty-eight radiation treatments?
A somber doctor reported, "Instead of the expected 90% shrinkage, the tumor has grown 30% *larger.*" As if zapped by a stun gun, the news paralyzed our response. A few seconds ticked by in silence. *No!* my mind raged, *this had to be a mistake!* After the predictions and all the suffering, how could this be? Yet the large area of blackened skin on her lower back from the radiation made it obvious *minimal damage to other tissue* hadn't been true either.

Our hearts limped through the moments as we absorbed the shock. We sat speechless as the doctor explained she was dying and immediately admitted her to the hospital.

> *Uhg!* Radiation turned out to be such a huge mistake.

The weekend became frightening as Esther started swelling from head to toe. The MRI revealed the enlarged tumor now pressed into her ureters and the kidneys were shutting down.

◎◎◎

The sudden cold symptoms of a leaky nose and scratchy throat left me fidgeting at my own doctor's appointment the next day. They were nothing compared to the ache of separation from Esther at such a critical time, but I couldn't risk exposing her.

> Seth spent the night at the hospital with her and wrote the following e-mail to a friend:

***Bad news,** the doctor said the 28 horrible treatments of radiation did not work at all.*

***Bad news,** in fact the tumor grew an inch or two which stymied the doctor.*

***Bad news,** her kidneys are being blocked again and is why the nausea and bloating.*

***Bad news,** he is admitting her to the hospital immediately.*

Bad news, *she will have to wear a urine bag.*

Bad news, *the doctor says she is terminal.*

This is **part** *of the hard truth, but it is not **all** the truth. God knows all the truth about how this horror story fits into 'All things work together for good, to them that love God, to those who are called according to His Purpose.'*

I'm trying to do my part and shout into the darkness…

"I BELIEVE!"

Seth's steadfast faith amazed me in the midst of these devastating events.

REFLECT

Have you ever felt deceived? Have you ever despaired? How do you find hope when like a rug, it trips you and you fall, and fall hard?

APPLY

Songs of praise and the pure eternal Word of God is the shot of adrenalin to sustain you.

Deuteronomy 31:8, *It is the Lord who goes before you. He will be with you; he will not leave you or forsake you. Do not fear or be dismayed.*

Isaiah 41:10, *…fear not, for I am with you; I will strengthen you, I will help you, I will uphold you with my righteous right hand.*

PRAYER

Dear Father, I feel abandoned and bereft, and like Seth, all I know to do is to shout into the darkness and say, *"I BELIEVE!"*

Chapter 31

Romeo's Return

Suddenly, the door to the hospital room burst open and there stood Romeo. The air crackled with apprehension and alarm. An angry challenging man staked his claim at Esther's bedside stating a lawyer friend helped track her down.

"Why didn't you tell me she was in the hospital?" Romeo demanded.

"Esther requested us not to," Seth replied.

Romeo had called the night before Esther's doctor appointment regarding the radiation results. Muting the phone, I'd asked Esther, "Do you want to tell him about your doctor's visit in the morning?"

Resolute, she responded, "No! I will deal with him when I'm ready."

Now, as we watched the scene unfold with Romeo, I felt Esther surrender—a trapped prey with no more energy to deal with the conflict. The radiation report had crushed her spirit.

The next ten days, Seth stayed at the hospital—so did Romeo.

Intense!

Seth knew how much a patient needed an advocate. Romeo, with a different mindset, saw no need for it. Seth questioned all medical procedures and caught more than one error which saved Esther unnecessary pain and complications. Medical staff are human, overworked, and make mistakes. On the wall next to the nurse's white board, a sign *encouraged* patients and caregivers to ask questions.

The first time in seven months, Esther's friend, Vera, came to the hospital to see her. She'd stayed away due to her fear of Romeo. However, when Vera saw his angry attacks on us and the dissension between him and our family, she stepped into the fray and became a forceful mediator to help bring peace.

That evening with Esther present, Vera assumed the role of arbitrator and encouraged Seth and Romeo to verbally lay out all their issues with each other. A long night of conciliation resulted. Shortly after midnight, Seth chose the route of humility and said to Romeo, "Yes, maybe we should have involved you more in the process."

He offered his hand. A handshake and tenuous peace resulted.

Seth said, "When I glanced at Esther's relaxed countenance, I knew I'd done the right thing."

I entered Esther's hospital room two days later and a perceptible harmony still held. Faces were relaxed and conversation amiable. Peace soothed my wobbly emotions.

During the ten days at the hospital, nephrostomy tubes were inserted into each ureter through Esther's back to drain her kidneys. Two blood transfusions were given along with I.V.'s and meds. Fever, nausea, and vomiting started the following weekend and pain shots had to be doubled in strength. She was to go home on Saturday, but inability to take pain pills kept her there another week.

Doctors were surprised at how quickly her kidney function returned and Esther chose to try some chemo treatments the next week. First a full body CAT scan was ordered to see if any additional cancer was present. Besides the inoperable tumor in the sacral plexus they found none. Surgery was considered to remove all remaining organs not necessary for survival, but later decided she was too weak and unstable.

I thought, *can this journey get any more gruesome?*

One evening Esther's sister, Jayne, visited her at the hospital and brought clothes, books, and requested items to her. She witnessed Romeo as he began the character assassination of our family to his international friends and moms of his students who had gathered to visit. Jayne sat stunned as Romeo told them we had kidnapped Esther, taken her phone and not allowed her to contact him. Many of her Russian friends had visited her at our home over the past months and knew this was untrue. His statements were bizarre and irrational. Jayne was disturbed by Esther's silence when she didn't speak up and come to our defense.

Later when I heard of Esther's silence, it cut deep, so I asked her, "Why, didn't you defend us?"

She said, "If I don't make him sound good, he gets angry."

The next week, I sat on a thin padded bench in Esther's hospital room as she and Romeo listened to her oncologist. "Esther, you are dying and I see only two options. Go into hospice where they will manage your pain and keep you comfortable. This could give you a few more months. Or, you could choose more chemo which might give you up to a year."

The doctor left the room. Romeo turned toward Esther, "Whatever you do, don't go into hospice. All they can do is give you morphine until it doesn't work anymore and then you will die an excruciating death." Shocked horror filled her face.

I knew five hospice workers personally and nothing was further from the truth.

Later, I explained, "Esther, when you leave the hospital, your Dad and I have to get help from hospice if you come back to our house. People involved in hospice are some of the most caring and compassionate people alive. Dad and I want to make sure you are taken care of in the best way possible. We're worn out and need the support. Hospice would just be a resource for us. It *is* associated with last stages of life, but people improve and are dismissed from their care also. You will be in our home, not a hospice facility."

Esther refused hospice. Besides the threatening description Romeo had given, maybe choosing hospice felt like giving up. She had such a strong belief God would miraculously heal her. A strong little warrior, she clung to life tenaciously.

REFLECT

Have you ever had to make a life and death choice between two equally unpleasant options?

APPLY

Let God's word, wisdom and peace dictate your path.

Your soul can be all right, even when everything in your world is all wrong.

Read: First Peter 1:3-9 NIV

PRAYER

Dear Heavenly Father,

Thank you for giving me a *living hope* through Jesus' resurrection. No matter the trial or suffering, your Word promises I have an imperishable inheritance waiting for me in heaven. Help me keep my eyes on your bigger picture regardless of the grief or trial. You are refining my faith which you say is of more worth than gold and will result in glory and honor when Jesus is revealed. Even though I can't see you now, my heart can be filled with inexpressible joy.

Chapter 32

March Madness and a Baptism

An emotional roller coaster filled the month of March 2016.

An unkept, dirty home and an unrepaired refrigerator caused Esther to refuse to go to her house after she left the hospital. Romeo moved her into a high-end hotel nearby. Financially, an unsustainable choice.

Vera, back in town from her business travels, spent hours searching for an extended-stay hotel. After an all-day-search, she announced, "I've found *one* affordable place that's perfect for Esther's needs." She brought Romeo the information brochure with instructions to call immediately. She knew it wouldn't stay available long at half the cost and only ten minutes from the hospital.

Romeo took no action.

Frail and worn out, Esther's negative reactions to her first chemo treatment were immediate. This set a stage of tension as she expressed her desire to be baptized.

As a young teen and involved with her church youth group, the question of baptism came up. Some friends chided, "Esther, unless you're baptized you won't go to heaven."

"That's not true! Salvation is through my personal faith in Christ alone," she responded. Her friends were adamant they were right and concerned she wouldn't go to heaven. So, Esther in her plucky way stated, "Oh yes I will—just watch me. I won't be baptized but I *will* meet you in heaven!"

The year before her cancer returned, she'd heard a sermon which stirred her heart with a desire to be baptized. Her beliefs hadn't changed, but she felt now was the right time.

When the subject of Esther's baptism emerged, Romeo became restless and agitated. To keep peace, Seth and I treaded lightly when it came to decisions regarding her health care, or otherwise. At Esther's request, we helped her search for a church with a baptismal. In great anger, Romeo came at Seth and me demanding we drop all talk of baptism. We were not to even say the word *baptism*. Peace for Esther—our main goal, we backed off.

Relational issues with Romeo and our family flared again.

The weekend of March 16, 2016, Esther became weak and listless. We didn't know if she'd make it through the weekend. She surprised everyone Monday morning when she woke up with an appetite and energy. After a good breakfast she focused her energy on her baptism. To be immersed concerned her because of the risk of infection, so she considered another option. Personally contacting the Care Network at her church, she scheduled a simple baptism to take place in her hotel room. A simple pitcher of water and a large empty bowl would suffice.

Taking full charge of this event she sent out the following online invitation:

Hello my dear friends, I am being baptized here in my hotel room Wednesday, March 20, 2016 at 2 p.m. I realize many of you will be at work, but this was the only time the Care Network team could come. I have been a Christian for such a long time and love God with all my heart, so I wanted to publicly profess my faith with friends and family, as God has been nudging my spirit to do so.

Thank you for all your tremendous love and support as I fight this battle.

Love,

Esther

Our family sat in shock when Romeo asked to speak to the group gathered after her baptism. He proceeded to share how he and Esther had anticipated this event eagerly and how it was one of the greatest moments of their lives. He continued to speak with silken-worded eloquence for several minutes. His words seemed so sincere and were artfully spoken, I thought, "Have I totally misunderstood this man?" It felt like I'd been interacting with Mr. Hyde, when suddenly Dr. Jekyll appeared.

Later, as I spoke with my oldest daughter, Jayne, she expressed what Seth and I had thought. "What in the world just happened? Have I missed something?" She was shocked at Romeo's words after he'd shut us all down the previous week. She said, "If I'd been one of the people in the room with no prior knowledge, I would have believed every word." Jayne discerns deception quickly and realized this man needed to be in control and manipulation was his tool.

Regardless, a sweet celebration beyond what Esther thought possible in a hotel room was enjoyed by twenty-three people who came with less than twenty-four-hour notice during work hours. Certainly, a grace to all, and a testimony to the influence of her life. Although physically spent at the end of the ceremony, a joyful heart was expressed by her glowing countenance and beautiful smile.

After the room emptied of guests, the presence of a darkness became a palpable entity.

REFLECT

Have you ever confronted an impossible situation and then watched as everything fell beautifully into place? Have you ever had an event where everything fell apart?

APPLY

Visualization is a powerful force. It can change your day; it can change your life. Write out Philippians 4:4-8 NIV on 3x5 cards. Print it out and post it beside the mirror in your bathroom. Saturate your mind and heart with these beautiful words of joy and hope.

Always be full of joy in the Lord. I say it again—rejoice!
Let everyone see that you are considerate in all you do.
Remember, the Lord is coming soon.
Don't worry about anything;
instead, pray about everything.
Tell God what you need,
and thank him for all he has done.
Then you will experience God's peace,
which exceeds anything we can understand.
His peace will guard your hearts and minds
as you live in Christ Jesus.
Finally, brothers, whatever is true, whatever is right,
whatever is pure, whatever is lovely, whatever is
admirable—if anything is excellent or praiseworthy—
think about such things.

PRAYER

Dear Heavenly Father, I choose to tuck these words from Philippians deep into the inner recesses of my mind and heart so encouragement and peace can heal my inner and outer broken world.

Chapter 33

Smile Crusher

A blood-curdling scream ripped the air startling everyone into action. The disparity of the prior moment when Esther's face glowed with pure joy and peace from her baptism, couldn't have been more extreme. The hotel room, now occupied by Seth, Romeo, Esther and me became a battle ground. Romeo rushed into the restroom Esther had entered moments before. The sound of hysterical crying caused my heart to race. Romeo came out and said, "Esther needs you!"

I entered and quickly scanned her bloody clothes, and what appeared to be a large mass of raw liver in the commode. All sorts of scenarios flashed through my traumatized mind. I wondered, *Was it possibly an organ from her body? A piece of her liver or kidney? Could that even be possible?* My quivering fingers grabbed the nearest makeshift tool—a plastic drinking straw to probe the mass. As my reasoning ability returned, I realized it was probably a huge mass of coagulated blood. I calmed her down with reassuring words and helped her get cleaned up and changed into fresh clothing.

After 5 p.m., and with doctors gone for the day, it was obvious she needed to be taken straight to the emergency room only two blocks away.

The spike in the emotional atmosphere of the hotel room caused Romeo to become verbally abusive as he started blaming us for an unrelated situation which occurred two weeks before when an ill-prepared nurse caused Esther an unnecessary night of pain. We knew of it but had nothing to do with it. False accusations had become a common form of divisiveness. Rather than providing a loving, caring atmosphere for healing, he established a toxic, combative situation of husband against parents, and Esther torn between loyalties. This happened often during the last weeks of her life.

Incredulous, I looked at him and said, "Your wife needs medical attention *now*, and you want to discuss *that*?" He wouldn't let up. I urged him to go out in the hall with us and talk—away from Esther. He would not, and by this time Seth recognized his tactics and left the room. The door to the hotel room was open and Seth yelled, "Please get out of there!" My feet felt frozen in place; my heart wrung with pain. How could I leave her so broken? Yet, as I glanced at Esther and saw her beautiful joy from the baptism being destroyed—I left.

Seth and I waited in the parking lot to make sure Romeo took her to the E.R. After a few minutes, we noticed his car leaving, but couldn't see if Esther was with him. Then he turned in the *opposite* direction of the hospital. Astonished, I said to Seth, "Surely, he didn't leave her alone!" Yet, what we knew of Romeo, compelled us to return to her room. Her solitary figure lay on the bed. We took her the short distance to the E.R. where they gave her IV's of fluids and pain meds and then released her.

Later, back at the hotel, I flushed Esther's PICC lines, a task I'd only done once before. I had almost finished when Esther's close friend came in bringing dinner. I gave a soft laugh as I greeted her, "Look at me, I'm in nurses training." She chuckled, then let us know she would take the night shift until Romeo returned.

Still emotionally wrung dry of energy from the earlier altercation, Seth and I left to make the familiar hour plus trip home. We arrived with bone-aching weariness, a common companion in this parallel universe we lived in.

© © ©

I jerked awake from my deep, exhausted sleep about midnight. Esther's name lit up my cell phone.

"Marmie, after you left, I experienced some extreme pain and became so frightened. You forgot to reopen the right PICC line when you flushed them earlier."

Devastated, I then remembered her friend had come in with supper; the interruption in the process had sidetracked me. Certainly, an honest mistake, but it caused her more suffering on a day that should have been full of joy and celebration. Would this nightmare never end?!

The next day dawned way too early. I checked my e-mails before I started working on student plans for the day.

A startling e-mail from Romeo sent my world into chaos once again.

REFLECT

Have you ever felt like Job where one calamity after another pummeled you? Since you're reading this book, you've most likely experienced grief or known someone who has. How can a day start out so beautiful and end up so hideous? How do you survive?

APPLY

This is where a support team of prayer warriors and hands-on-help are a critical part of your journey. Even if you're not presently in a church, reach out to one or a community group, neighbors, or even AA friends who may already be supporting you.

There are people whose gifting and joy is to help others. Don't withhold *their* blessing. Humble yourself and *ask* for help.

PRAYER

Dear Heavenly Father,

Asking for help is so hard. Help me to lay down my pride and reach out to others. To be vulnerable is scary and humbling, yet I realize even Jesus, God in the flesh, had His own group called disciples. Even if no one steps forward to help, I remember you're called Emmanuel. God *with us*. You are *with me* and will never abandon me. You will provide all I need.

Chapter 34

Wounding the Wounded

Well aimed fiery darts hit their intended mark of our exposed, struggling hearts. Lies, exaggeration and reprimands filled the e-mail before me. To further humiliate—it had been shared with nine other people and written with the impression Esther had been the co-author and in full agreement. In truth, Esther knew nothing about it. Not wanting to cause her more distress, I didn't reveal to her the full contents of the e-mail.

A livid, angry grief warred in my soul all that day. I wanted to lash out, defend, and set the record straight! I thought, "How do I speak truth into this without sounding unloving, pathetic or guilty?" A sleepless night added to my anxiety and tumultuous inner contortions.

Prostrate and wrung dry by noon Saturday, I relinquished any adequacy to solve this. I cried out, "Holy Spirit fill me with Your mind. Please bring Your clarity, love and wisdom to me. How do I react to this mess?"

The words of Hebrews 4:15-16 rescued me...

For we do not have a high priest who is unable to empathize with our weaknesses,

but we have one who has been tempted in every way,

just as we are—yet he did not sin.

Let us then approach God's throne of grace with confidence,

so that we may receive mercy and find grace to help us in our time of need.

Comforted, I relaxed in His presence. Then a scene came to mind of Jesus before Pilate. The religious leaders, the priests and elders were accusing Jesus of heresy and demanding His death. Puzzled, Pilate became confused by Jesus silence. The setting seemed so out of context for my situation at first. Then, spiritual insight came and I thought, *I'm to remain silent and not argue our case.* The Lord's way—so against the grain of my flesh instincts.

I pressed "All", as I sent a simple response to Romeo's e-mail:

"I will simply say, everything Seth and I have done throughout the last ten months has been from a heart of the deepest love one can have for their child, and only acted upon at Esther's request."

"If you'd like to speak with us personally, we'd be happy to talk with you. We seek only to walk in the sweet presence and peace of our Lord."

Seth & Marla

No one responded.

REFLECT

Do you see what God did right in the midst of my anger with a heart full of justified pain and a desire to lash back and be validated?

APPLY

When we let our pain bring us to our knees and in honesty cry out to the Lord, He will speak to our spirit and direct us. When we've made a habit of studying His Word, it just makes it easier. He'll communicate with us whatever it takes in such painful but honest circumstances. Just know the answer will always take us to and through the cross of Jesus.

PRAYER

Dear Heavenly Father, once again I come and bring my pain and confusion to You. When I focus on your sinless purity, yet you were willing to go to the cross to pay for my anger, wrath and vengeance toward my enemies, I'm stopped in my tracks and choose to bow to your ways of peace.

Chapter 35

Angel or Adversary?

Grief, fear, and twisted faith converged into a religious nightmare as the month of March advanced. Behind the scenes, a sinister spirit worked to cause Esther and our family great sorrow over the next five months.

A few friends and new acquaintances, zealous in their desire to see Esther miraculously healed, brought an imbalance of false claims into play. Sound theology became distorted with their own personal needs and agendas. Caught up with these passions, they brought new elements to further litter our life-scape with more confusion and pain.

The fragility of Esther's health, intense pain, and strong pain meds created a vulnerability to such claims, creating false expectations. But—who am I kidding? I also desired and prayed for a miraculous healing. Grasping at hope and God's mercy became part of this journey.

Cecelia, a well-intentioned, self-appointed healer and prayer warrior entered Esther's life mid-March 2014. She'd heard about Esther through her church. We were surprised someone would come pray for a stranger and offer to donate financially as well.

When I first heard Cecelia pray, I thought, *How awesome. This woman could pray down angel armies— she is so commanding and articulate—maybe God has sent us our own warrior angel.* On mornings when we'd come to visit Esther, we'd often hear Cecelia's powerful voice echoing down the halls as soon as the elevator opened.

Cecelia told me the story of her father's cancer. Desperate to save her Dad's life, she told God she would give Him hers if He would save him. Because her father survived, she dedicated her life to God with a mission to pray for the sick. Her faithfulness and good intentions were undeniable as she came daily to pray with Esther for several months.

I questioned Esther, "How do you feel about Cecelia coming *every* day?

"Marmie, I know her method and beliefs differ from mine, but prayer comforts me."

Mornings when I would arrive at the hotel, I'd walk past the breakfast area and notice Romeo and Cecelia in deep conversation. I had no question about Cecelia's sincerity, but gradually as she bonded with Romeo a harsh demanding edge entered her prayers and her demeanor toward our family became hostile.

Complications and increased physical agony placed Esther in the hospital again. It had taken all day to get her pain under control. Late afternoon she drifted into peaceful sleep. Standing outside Esther's room, my daughter, Jayne and I, noticed Cecelia headed our way. I said, "We need to insist she not disturb Esther." We planted ourselves firmly in front of the door. The fixed set of Cecelia's jaw and determined eyes should have alerted us, but the rude abruptness as she ignored our pleas and pushed her way into Esther's room shocked us. Cecelia demanded Esther had to be awake when she prayed so she could consciously fight for her life. She strongly opposed hospice care as well since they sedated cancer patients. Romeo supported Cecelia in this cruel demand.

At times it felt like I'd been placed in a straitjacket and made to watch an evil plot of torture unfold, my daughter the victim. Powerless to keep Esther safe, it exposed in me a frightening and fierce mother's love.

Perspective came when I thought of how much my Father God had loved me to allow His *perfect* Holy Son to be flayed and crucified for me. A whole new level of appreciation for His sacrifice overwhelmed my heart. Once again, words of an old hymn warmed and held me gently. *Amazing love, how can it be, that thou my God couldst die for me?*

God made him who had no sin to be sin for us,

so that in him we might become the righteousness of God.

2 Corinthians 5:21 NIV

REFLECT

Have you been given unwanted advice by someone with tunnel vision who had no idea of the bigger picture and what you were going through?

APPLY

When there's so many moving parts to a sticky situation it's hard to see the big picture when it's so close and personal. Since Esther had chosen to stay under Romeo's headship, to have opposed him in her limited physical state would have added more tension and unrest to her situation. Sometimes there is no "best way," just practical wisdom of how to best dodge the bullets.

PRAYER

Dear Heavenly Father, show me your ways as I choose to hide your words of wisdom in my heart and mind.
Proverbs 3:21 – 23 The Message
...guard Clear Thinking and Common Sense with your life; don't for a minute lose sight of them. They'll keep your soul alive and well, they'll keep you fit and attractive. You'll travel safely, you'll neither tire nor trip.

Chapter 36

Sabotage

March 2016

Seth and I were scheduled to stay with Esther at the hotel from 10 a.m. to 2 p.m. We hadn't seen her since the baptism a week prior and longed for some quality time together.

As soon as we arrived, Romeo sent Seth to pick up some medical supplies. What should have been a fifteen-minute errand turned into a wild goose chase of three hours.

A knock on the door disrupted Cecelia, Esther's prayer warrior, who'd arrived earlier. Esther's friend entered with fresh juices. I thought, *how kind of her to do that on her way to work.* She introduced us to a young woman who'd entered with her. She had just arrived from overseas for her first visit to the U. S. At only 19 years old she was said to have a special gift as a prophetess.

They didn't leave.

The hotel room became crowded.

Like sand in an hour-glass, my precious time with Esther ebbed away. I became annoyed. When Romeo made no hint of leaving either, a wariness settled into my spirit. His condemning e-mail after her baptism had occurred only a week before.

The guests gathered around Esther and after a bit of stilted conversation, Esther announced, "I want to go for a walk." A clever maneuver on her part to get some time together. I grabbed her walker and assisted her out the door.

I thought it beyond odd, when the visitor followed us into the hall. It felt like I had a part in a twisted play, except I didn't have the script or know the plot. I thought, *has she been instructed to shadow us?*

Resisting paranoia, I engaged her in small talk and asked about her life. Queen of the afterthought, I should have requested time alone with my daughter. But taken off guard, I couldn't make sense of the situation.

We'd just returned to the room and another knock at the door revealed Jack and Candy, an older couple who were in leadership positions of a former church we'd attended. Esther and Romeo were in a group with them when they dated, but only had surface knowledge of Romeo's true character. Jack seemed enamored with

Romeo's history in the military and his martial art skills. I think he saw Romeo as the perfect renaissance man.

Previous conflict with them during Esther's convalescence at our home made it clear the events of this morning were no coincidence.

◎◎◎

In February when Jack and Candy volunteered to take Esther to a doctor appointment. I thought, *Wow! Esther must be very dear to them to make a six-hour round trip,* as they had moved a good distance away. But she was blind-sided as to their true purpose.

After the doctor appointment, Jack and Candy treated Esther to dinner so they could *visit* with her. Instead, they shamed her for staying with us, her parents, telling her she belonged at home with her husband. Their distorted mindset led to *preaching at her*—accusing her of being *too sensitive*. Yet, were unwilling to hear her side of the story about the abusive relationship.

When they brought her home many hours later, oblivious to her agony from not having taken any pain meds with her, she'd been physically and emotionally beaten to the ground. She begged, "Please, Marmie, *never* let them near me again!" It took two days to relieve her pain.

◎◎◎

Their visit at this moment was no happenstance either. I sat stunned as Jack delivered a thirty-minute sermon on the sanctity of marriage and how the wife should submit to her husband. I filled the role of the soft target as Seth would have seen the ruse and walked out. (It seemed convenient they had placed themselves in front of the only exit door.)

Therefore, Seth's assigned errand to find the elusive medical supplies gave Romeo opportunity to put me in my place and Esther in hers. Having been deceived, Jack and Candy were unaware they'd been *played*. For two years after Esther's memorial service, Romeo would not respond to any of Jack's attempts to contact him. Jack had served Romeo's purpose.

When Seth returned from his ridiculous three-hour errand, we went to the lobby to eat the salads he'd brought and I explained the morning's events. I went back to say goodbye to Esther, where we had five minutes alone. Outraged with Romeo, she said she had vented her fury while we were downstairs eating. As my soul throbbed with the sadness of our lost time together, I left to go to work. My heart a mass of misery.

I held my tongue as I knew Esther would pay the price after we were gone. Anything I'd say in front of these people who already thought we were in the wrong wouldn't have changed their minds. Romeo had a honed skill for manipulating people and thrived on contention— a deadly combination.

During the surreal moments of those few hours, Father God felt so present. What happened was so hurtful at a time when we were struggling just to breathe and keep our heads above water. But even as my emotions churned and my heart felt crushed, scripture tucked away from the past came to mind and brought great comfort.

And the peace of God, which transcends all
understanding,
will guard your hearts and your minds in Christ Jesus.
Philippians 4:7 NIV

With faith comes the opportunity of *choice* and this peace comes when we *choose* to give the *sacrifice of praise.* Peace in the midst of pain is an earmark of the Holy Spirit's presence.

My fractured heart found more healing through recording artist, Mandisa's, beautiful song…

A Broken Hallelujah

With my love and sadness
I come before You Lord
My heart's in a thousand pieces

Maybe even more

Yet I trust in this moment

You're with me somehow

You've always been faithful

So, Lord even now

When all that I can sing,

is a broken hallelujah
When my only offering

is shattered praise

I discovered when I spoke or sang such words of faith to the Lord through pain, gritted teeth, and tear-drenched voice—it created a tear in the fabric of heaven and supernatural peace would cocoon my soul, releasing my wings to soar above the grief.

Once again, I *experienced* Emmanuel, God *with* me.

REFLECT

Have you experienced the friends of Job in the traumas of *your* life? The ones who start out comforting but end up accusing?

APPLY

Wise friends have three qualities: Love. Knowledge. Personal humility. Look for these traits in those you seek and accept guidance from.

When in grief beware of anyone's advice containing: *Should, Shouldn't, You better, It's time you, I think you should.*

* By an act of faith...Cry out your pain, build your faith, and comfort your heart by listening to the complete song: "A Broken Hallelujah" by Mandisa.

PRAYER

Dear Heavenly Father, it's good to know you are fine with my tears. My brokenness is not hidden from you. I know you understand, because you've been there. There's no sabotage, sorrow, or betrayal I can experience worse than what you went through for me.

Chapter 37

Endurance

April brought the expected turbulence of spring weather along with a maelstrom of new medical challenges. The inoperable tumor in Esther's sacral plexus left few options, so she chose more chemo treatments hoping to survive long enough for a miraculous healing.

Potent odors accosted our nose as we entered Esther's hotel room. She consumed less and less food, so with little to digest her nausea brought up quarts of bitter green bile. Nephrostomy tubes still extended from her back to allow her kidneys to drain. The death spiral seemed obvious.

As if that wasn't enough to deal with—after the cruel visit by Jack and Candy my counselor advised me against being alone in Romeo's presence. He would not attack or cause contention in anyone else's company so I came with a personal friend, or waited until Esther notified me she was alone.

But by mid-April after three chemo treatments the tumor shrank 30%. We were hopeful and excited. She'd lost so much weight though, the Dr. put her on a TPN machine (nutritional supplements) 24 hours a day. She pushed a big bag of liquids around on a pole all day and slept with it at night. It appeared to be a caricature of a skinny man with a big belly, so we called him Charlie.

The rest of April and May became a blur of ups and downs, chemo sessions, tests, scans and desperate measures to stay alive. Mid-May Esther's nephrostomy tubes were replaced with stents. Relational contentions mounted.

In late May, I came to visit and Esther told me Romeo would be gone over Memorial Day weekend for a soccer tournament. She pleaded, "Marmie, I know I'm hooked up to this TPN machine and urine bag, but could we work out a way for me to come home for the weekend?" Thrilled she'd asked, my mind spun with plans to make it happen.

Unexpectedly, Romeo entered the room with Cecelia.

Esther asked, "Since you'll be gone for the weekend, I want to stay with my parents."

Indignant, Romeo shot back, "I can't believe you would even consider such a thing!"

"This is *my* idea!" Esther snapped. "*I* asked Mom if I could come home. *I* need to get out of this room, to have something to look forward to, and do something I enjoy!"

He sneered, "Aren't you afraid they'll put you in hospice? Can't you see, they're trying to take you away from me again?"

Even amidst Esther's protests, Romeo insisted I had instigated the invitation.

Cecelia entered the fray with hospice comments of her own. "Esther, I prayed for a woman in hospice and she died because she couldn't stay awake to claim her healing. If you go into hospice, they'll keep you drugged and you won't be able to stay awake to fight to live. You *must* stay conscious."

Like a lawyer making closing comments Romeo paced the room as he continued a stream of accusations directed at me. "You're such a hypocrite, but soon your mask will come off and the truth come out!" He continued with innuendo and unsubstantiated accusations of our interference with Esther's care.

I cried, "Enough! I'm leaving." I looked at Esther— so broken. I reconsidered and told her, "I'll be downstairs. Call me when you'd like me to come back."

I'd been out walking the trail around a pond behind the hotel when Esther called for me to return. I crossed the parking lot where Cecelia had just opened her car door.

She confronted me, "You need to back off. Esther shouldn't be at your house. It's wrong. She should obey her husband!"

I sighed as once again this *out of context* quote pummeled us and Esther once again. The interference of so many who were ignorant of the truth astounded me. I wanted to deck her right there. I tried reasoning with her but without success. I saw Cecelia in a whole new light: immature in her faith, legalistic, and speaking into situations she didn't understand. Clearly, Romeo had poisoned her against us.

Interjecting advice into someone's life when you don't have all the information is unwise.

As I re-entered the hotel room, Romeo immediately tried to bait me into further arguments. I said firmly, "I'll be glad to meet with you and a counselor, but not in front of Esther." As excruciating as cancer is to experience in someone you love, the continual shredding of our family's heart—a slow and agonizing execution—felt almost as painful.

Esther immediately requested we go for a walk. Although a snail-paced shuffle for her, we made our way to the gazebo behind the hotel. We prayed together and our hearts calmed. I asked a simple question: "If you could wave a magic wand, what would your world look like?"

Her rapid-fire response, "To not be married!" followed by a defeated—"but, I am."

Romeo agreed for Esther to do short outings with us from the hotel over the Memorial Day weekend. Crestfallen with no energy to fight, Esther caved to his wishes. To avoid more conflict, we made the daily journey.

Seth, ever an attentive dad, made Esther a thick foam pallet, covered with a favorite patchwork quilt, complete with pillows for our day trips. I packed healthy picnic lunches and we found peaceful outdoor landscapes for her makeshift bed where she immersed herself in the splendor of God's beautiful world.

Sun-infused breezes swirled fresh spring air over our upturned faces as new green leaves fluttered and danced. Memorial Day weekend found us feeding ducks by the pond, exploring a local Nature Center at a slow hobble, and basking in sunshine beside a lake. Treasured moments for us all.

I don't know how I peeled myself off my bed every morning. Most days began with my body bonded to the carpet crying out to God for strength. I claimed His promises, fed on the Psalms, and sang out raspy tear-drenched hymns and worship songs. He *never* failed to comfort me with His peace. *The Lord is close to the broken-hearted and saves those who are broken in spirit.* I experienced it time after time.

I found a poem by Sheila Walsh from her book, "In the Middle of the Mess." It still melts me into a puddle as she perfectly captures my experience during those early morning hours. Her words expressed the Lord's tender love for me. His love for you is the same.

Lord, I never knew you lived so close to the floor.

Every time I'm bowed down by this weight of grief,

I feel your hand on my head,

Your breath on my cheek,

Your tears on my neck.

You never tell me to pull myself together,

to stem the flow of many tears,

You simply stay by my side

For as long as it takes...close to the floor.

For you know when your faith is tested, your endurance
has a chance to grow.

James 1:3

REFLECT

Why is endurance so necessary in our faith-walk?

APPLY

Our Savior and example, Jesus, lived out endurance more than any other.

Why? I believe He modeled how to *trust* the Father even when life didn't make sense.

Study the inner life of Jesus:

> *I can do nothing on my own. I judge as God tells me.*
> *Therefore, my judgment is just, because I carry out the*
> *will of the one who sent me, not my own will.*
>
> John 5:30 NLT

There's a sequence to our faith-walk: first we *believe,* a consent of our mind; then comes *faith,* a choice of our will; and then *trust,* a commitment of the heart.

PRAYER

Dear Heavenly Father,

As your Son Jesus modeled how to walk out our own faith, I believe with my mind, by faith I choose to follow His example and commit to trust You from my heart. Without You I can accomplish *nothing.*

Chapter 38

God in the Land of the Living

June 14, 2016

I floated in the spaces between sleep and consciousness as light penetrated my leaden eyelids. My body—a hollow, numbed shell, I had emotionally flat-lined; I was alive, yet every cell felt desensitized. Terrified, I questioned, *"Am* I alive?"

Time suspended as I slid a leg over the edge of the bed and gingerly touched a toe to the floor. Like a slug, waiting for its body fluid to accumulate enough to move forward, my body followed as I stretched out flat beside the bed. Eyes wide with the surreal-ness of the moment, I spotted a favorite book leaning against the nightstand: *Get Out of That Pit,* by Beth Moore. How appropriate. My sloth-like hand inched it toward me and I turned to the last pages of the book for suggested scriptures and prayers where it referenced Psalm 27:13

Make me confident of this: I will see the goodness of the Lord in the land of the living.

I rasped, "Lord, I *need* to see your goodness today!"

The loud ringing startled me as three calls piggy-backed into my cell phone.

First, my friend and counselor called to check on me. Her gift of healing words flowed and lifted me as if spoken straight from the Savior's heart. Tears broke through the numbness as energy seeped into the cracks of my soul.

I returned the second call from my sister-in-law who had dealt with a similar heart-breaking family relationship. As we talked, I felt like she'd been living in my skin, because she'd experienced similar betrayals and trauma. The influence of someone understanding your pain brings powerful comfort. As she prayed and cried with me, her compassionate presence sparked new strength.

The third call came from my sister, who while on vacation, toured a beautiful historic chapel in Rhode Island. She felt burdened to pray and light lots of candles. Her spirit sensed my need.

The significance of these three calls at the same moment from three different areas across the country looped their love around my core. Renewed, I hung up after the last call and sat in a state of wonder. The timing, the gracious applicable words, the heavenly significance.

An explosion of joy erupted as my hands raised to heaven and I laughed aloud:

"Okay, God! I Get It!

You are *so personal*.

You *hear* me.

You *see* me.

You *care*.

These ladies were Your goodness to me today in the land of the living.

Hallelujah and Amen!''

Praise be to You, Lord, for showing Your wonderful love to me when I was besieged and felt cut off from Your sight. You heard my cry for mercy.

Psalm 31:21-22 NIV

REFLECT

Sometimes in our deep pain our minds and even our physical senses numb out. All that seems left is our deadened present. What then?

APPLY

Keep God's Word close by. On the nightstand, near your favorite spot of respite, in your prayer closet. If you don't have a place, create one in the less stressful moments. Print out the lyrics to favorite praise songs and hymns. Post scriptures on the wall close to your bed, on the bathroom mirror, over the kitchen sink. This is a war; your heart, mind, and soul are the targets. You have the armor and the weapon. The truths of God's Word. Draw near to God, resist the devil, he has to flee. Jesus already won these battles for you. Claim His victory in your trial and pain.

PRAYER

Dear Heavenly Father,

I choose to claim the hard-fought victory you've already won for me through your Son. Even if all I can say is "Jesus, Help me!" I will prepare by keeping the truths of your word in my heart and at my fingertips.

Chapter 39

A Myrtle Beach Birthday

From a restless sleep, I shot straight up like a soldier snapping to attention. The *Oh no! and What ifs?* bombarded my mind.

By June the machines and tubes connected to Esther had been removed. The doctor met with our family, his voice laced with empathy as he explained, "There's nothing more we can do." He turned to Esther, "Go spend time with the people you love and do the things you enjoy. It'd be best to use hospice to assist and help manage your pain at a facility or in your home."

We had heard this death diagnosis before in March when the MRI results were given after her twenty-eight sessions of unsuccessful radiation. Yes, we were now jolted into facing this reality again but we were not undone as we were the first time. Throughout her illness, especially after the Lord spoke to me from Isaiah 57 the previous summer, I'd been ripped apart by the brutal possibility of her death. But I knew the end game; live or die she *would win.* The prayer for me now became, *how does this fit into your bigger plan, Lord? Somehow, I know you will bring beauty from these ashes.*

Still, this vicious news ripped open an abyss of fierce dread and sorrow. No matter how you wrap death with faith, prayers or scripture, it's a cruel process.

A few days before Esther's birthday, smiling and more animated than I'd seen her for a good while, she said, "Guess what Marmie? Heidi's taking me to Myrtle Beach for my birthday!" A mixture of emotions orbited my core as Esther expressed her excitement. Although thrilled for her, the news crushed me to think we wouldn't spend her last birthday together.

The "What ifs?" which awakened me and set my heart racing were valid. If she left on this trip, I may not be with her if she passed, the trauma to Heidi if she died while in South Carolina, the complicated bureaucratic systems getting her back across state lines, plus the expense could be daunting and overall heartbreaking. These complications were not unfounded as the charge to get my mother to another state when she passed cost $10,000.

The previous day I'd sat beside Esther at a café; she labored for several hours to eat half a bagel sandwich. She reminded me of a baby bird with broken wings as I stroked her fuzzy nearly bald head. She didn't look like she'd be with us much longer. A beach trip felt daunting.

I berated myself as I thought, *why hadn't I taken her to the beach?* She'd wanted to go since her second cancer diagnosis. The time just never seemed right. Pressures to start treatments immediately, another doctor to see, another test result. I wouldn't have been brave enough to take her out of state in her present condition. But I'd also learned in this wild journey, things were often not what they seemed. Youth and lack of life experience on Heidi's part might be the only way she'd get there. I surrendered Esther to the only One who knew the future and trusted him to provide all she needed.

◎ ◎ ◎

A notification popped into my phone from Esther on her birthday. Heidi had gifted her with a floppy broadbrimmed hat, a new swim suit and purple cover-up. With her Audrey Hepburn-style sunglasses, Esther sported a big smile and her face radiated joy. I knew in that moment God had her in the palm of His hand.

Verification of this came later when my granddaughter, Cassi, burst through the front door, "Grammy, Grammy, did you see the light?" She shoved the picture on her phone under my nose. "It hasn't been photo-shopped either," she exclaimed.

I asked, "What do you mean?" I recognized the picture as the one of Esther on her birthday. Cassidy continued to insist I see the white glow surrounding Esther.

My mouth dropped in awe as my eyes focused and traced the aura of light bordering her.

Tears of joy fell as the Lord revealed how close He hovered over both Esther and me in our brokenness. His tender presence in the midst of suffering revealed once again my Emmanuel, God with us.

The LORD wraps himself in light as with a garment; he
stretches out the heavens like a tent.

Psalms 104:2

Esther's last birthday at Myrtle Beach

A container of God's love and light…Esther seemed to radiate His essence.

REFLECT

Have you been in a situation with walls on every side of you; trapped in a nightmare you didn't even create? How can that be for your good? Or if you *were* responsible, how does God want to use even that?

APPLY

The hard truth is, God uses trouble to transform us, whether we stumble into it unaware or create it by our own choices. It's in our darkest days we can experience our most intimate and profound moments with God. Our prayers become honest and authentic as there's no energy for cover-ups and superficial ones.

"When life is rosy,

we may slide by with knowing *about* Jesus,

with imitating him and quoting him and speaking of him.

But only in suffering will we *know* Jesus."

Joni Eareckson Tada

PRAYER

Heavenly Father,

John 16:33 says in this world I can expect trouble, but to take heart as you have overcome the world. I choose to walk with eyes of faith lifted toward you and through honest prayers come to *know* you.

Chapter 40

A Plea for Peace

It's impossible to go through the spiritual war I'd fought without sin affecting my own heart as well. The Lord's presence prodded me awake early July 2016. I'd learned to pay attention to His familiar twilight nudges. My thoughts spun with humbling conviction and led to examining my own heart. How could I move forward with all this anger and conflict churning below the surface?

I snatched my pencil and notepad from the bedside table and prayed as I wrote. I knew the ideas were from the Lord as they focused on personal humility. The exact opposite of my self-justification, angry thoughts, and belligerent heart.

Esther's life verses from Ephesians 6 scrolled unbidden through my mind. Her prayers and core desire were to see her family healed spiritually and to be at peace with each other. Spiritual warfare prayers for those she loved were encapsulated in Ephesians 6:10 NIV.

Finally, be strong in the Lord and in His mighty power.

Put on the full armor of God,

so that you can take your stand against the devil's schemes.

I unsheathed God's word in this moment of battle.

Submit yourselves therefore to God.

Resist the devil, and he will flee from you.

James 4:7 NIV

I'd experienced peace every time I prayed this aloud. The power of it left me in awe.

Encouraging scenarios emerged and condensed into one word—*Repentance.* Once again, on my face before the Lord with pleas and petitions for His guidance, the thought came, *maybe our greatest gift to Esther would be the miracle of allowing God to heal **us**—her family.* The perfect backdrop for her emotional, and possible physical healing.

Esther's health continued to plummet as the granules of her life spiraled through an hour glass of measured time; I needed to get this right. Live or die, to give her the gift of our peace with each other, would be the greatest present of all. As I began to write my personal plea to

Romeo for forgiveness and peace, I realized the vital need of presenting this with wisdom wrapped in humility.

When we reached Esther's hospital room later that morning, Romeo and Vera were already there. Seth and I loved on Esther a bit and settled in. After explaining my early morning time with the Lord, I read verses from Ephesians 6 and proceeded with my entreaty to make peace between us for Esther's sake.

A knock on the door interrupted me as I started to read. Cecelia, the lady who'd come daily to pray, peeked in. Tenuously, I asked her to come in. We needed peace with her as well.

I began again: "My goal today is to bring honor to the Lord Jesus, whom Esther loves and serves, and to honor her life as we proceed from here. Along with me, would you all allow the peace of God to rule in your heart from this point forward? There's been a lot of speculations, accusations, and judgments against each other. The stress it brings compromises Esther's well-being and therefore her ability to heal.

One focal point has been our judgments about each other's spiritual condition and walk with God. In truth, only God knows our hearts. Conflict also comes from the way we think God will heal Esther.

Romeo, just yesterday you accused Seth and me of not believing God's promises. Seth and I discussed this and have put into words what we believe. I wrote the following:

We absolutely believe and cry out consistently for God to heal Esther, but wisdom and compassion dictates we make her comfortable with as little pain as possible as we wait and pray for her healing. We have different views of hospice. I'm not here to argue about it, but I know God's power to heal is not thwarted because she's getting the merciful care she needs.

This morning my thoughts filled with the idea of bringing Esther the gift of our personal repentance, forgiveness, and kindness to each other. I realize I can't make that decision for anyone but myself, but maybe the greatest miracle the Lord desires, is to heal *us*. Maybe individually and corporately, we've allowed the enemy so much power because of our lack of personal humility and forgiveness toward each other. I think this is the best gift we can give Esther at this point."

I left Esther's bed where I'd been perched and went to kneel beside Romeo, and said, "You may think I hate you, but that is a lie. At times I've judged you, been angry, bitter, and held a self-righteous attitude. Please forgive my pride and a lack of love toward you. I care about you and desire peace between all of us. Can you receive that?"

I met resistance as he turned his body away from me and said, "Marla, you don't have to do this." I remained kneeling as I stared at the back of his head; he seemed incredulous, embarrassed, and resistant to my request. I glanced at Cecelia. Her countenance revealed disgust.

Dispirited, I sighed, rose, and went over to Esther. I felt I had carried out what God led me to do. Although drowsy from pain meds, I hoped Esther had caught enough of the conversation to know my heart and be encouraged.

The rest of the passage in Ephesians 6 completes Esther's life verses I'd read earlier:

For our struggle is not against flesh and blood, but against the rulers,
against the authorities, against the powers of this dark world
and against the spiritual forces of evil in the heavenly realms.

Therefore, put on the full armor of God,
so that when the day of evil comes,

you may be able to stand your ground,

and after you have done everything, to stand.

Stand firm then, with the belt of truth buckled around your waist,

with the breastplate of righteousness in place,

And with your feet fitted with the readiness

that comes from the gospel of peace.

In addition to all this, take up the shield of faith,

with which you can extinguish all the flaming arrows of the evil one.

Take the helmet of salvation and the sword of the Spirit,

which is the word of God. And pray in the Spirit on all occasions

with all kinds of prayers and requests.

With this in mind, be alert and always keep on praying

for all the Lord's people.

Ephesians 6:11-18 NIV

REFLECT

Have you ever been praying for God to do a work in others when all along He wanted to change your heart? Is he asking you to forgive someone and you've been resistant?

APPLY

In prayer there is a connection between what God does and what you do.
You can't get forgiveness from God, for instance, without also forgiving others.
If you refuse to do your part, you cut yourself off from God's part.
Matthew 6:14-15 The Message

Matthew 6 does not teach our eternal destiny is based on our forgiving other people; however, it does teach our relationship with God will be damaged if we refuse to pardon those who have offended us.

Matthew 6:12 *and forgive us our debts, as we also have forgiven our debtors.*

If in our day to day cleansing as we confess our sins to restore fellowship with our heavenly Father, yet withhold forgiveness from someone else is not only bizarre but hypocritical.

PRAYER

Dear Heavenly Father,

Help me to examine my own heart first and remember your forgiveness for me as you suffered and died the cruelest death on the cross. I desire to experience sweet communion with you and know the soul-rest that comes from forgiving my enemies.

Chapter 41

Rights Stripped

Mortified, Esther found herself alone in the middle of a tidal wave of nausea as she sat in the dining room of the upscale hotel. The embarrassing mess which followed left her thoroughly humiliated. Another degradation of this ugly disease.

Friends were helping less as they began to feel used and manipulated by Romeo to donate time and money to keep Esther in a financially untenable situation. Romeo, away at soccer practice didn't answer his phone. In desperation Esther called me. I lived an hour away so I called her friend who was located near the hotel. She came and assisted Esther back to her room.

When Romeo returned later, the friend confronted him: "Staying at this hotel is wrong and people are tired of being used and mistreated. If you'll leave the hotel *today*, my husband and I will pay the bill."

Volunteers came to the hotel, packed Esther's things and set her up at home. Friends offered to clean but were rejected by Romeo, so their home was not a pleasant space. The broken refrigerator from a year prior had never been repaired which made it hard to manage the meals brought in. Mice feces covered the floor from living room, to kitchen, to the sunroom. Only one person volunteered to help the following week, so Seth and I traded off every other day.

Esther's desire for a social life dwindled, so when several distant acquaintances came to see her she pleaded, "Marmie please make them go away; I just want to be with my family." I stepped outside and conveyed Esther's request. Romeo let them in but after a few awkward moments, they left.

@@@

The end of Esther's second week home, her friend, Vera, had been with her during the morning. Seth and I arrived at noon to take over her care. As I stepped from the car, Vera steered me away from the house and said, "I need to speak with you privately. I want you to know Romeo has been spreading rumors about you and Seth for quite some time now." As she shared the nature of the allegations, I felt like an elephant had landed on my chest. The severity of the accusations caused my stomach to pitch as fear, heartache, and indignation jumbled my nervous system into a wild panic. He'd accused Seth and me of horrible abuse to all three of our daughters. *Why? How could he spread such vile lies? How dare he!*

As Vera continued, I realized she also felt we were guilty. She had been taken in by the monstrous fabrications of Romeo. Words of blame followed, "You're the ones blocking Esther's healing. If you ask God's forgiveness Esther will be healed. I can recommend a church which has a specialized prayer ministry where you can go for help."

No matter what I said in our defense, she wouldn't listen.

Wow! I thought, *Our daughter is dying and you're accusing us of such disgraceful things?!* The evil swirled, slithered and compressed like a boa constrictor suffocating its prey. The unfathomable lies shocked and stung.

Then, I remembered Vera's false prophesy when she told us God had shown her Esther would be healed if she'd be baptized. It didn't happen. In the Old Testament, she would be labeled a false prophet and be stoned. Although small, the stones on the gravel driveway looked tempting. A short time later she left and Seth and I took over Esther's care.

☉☉☉

I'd been reading a pamphlet from the hospital, titled, "The Dying Experience," about the signs a person exhibits as death draws near. I saw them that day as Esther slipped in and out of consciousness. Confused speech, agitated arm movements, and numerous times she made picking motions with her hands like she had lint on her bedclothes. *Oh,* I thought, *if we only had the guidance and support of hospice, they could make this process so much easier.*

☉☉☉

Esther's friend, Heidi, and her mother arrived to provide care Friday evening through Saturday. To the best of our knowledge, we explained her meds and how to care for her, then left. The snail-paced weekend passed as we thought once again, *this nightmare can't get any worse.*

Sunday morning, back at Esther's home, our repeated rounds of knocking met with silence. Checking his cell phone, Seth found a text from Romeo. Esther had been taken to the ER and placed in ICU. Panic niggled as we rushed to the hospital, realizing she could slip away at any moment. As we entered the ER, Romeo strode past us with a leather binder holding official-looking documents.

I went to locate Esther to find out what happened. The critical issue—she'd lost all ability to swallow or speak. A sip of water at this point could cause her to drown. I shuddered at the thought. According to Romeo, she'd nodded yes when the doctor asked her if she wanted to continue her fight to live. We were skeptical of his claim. There was talk of more chemo and a blood transfusion. If her heart stopped they'd determined she would not be resuscitated as the electrical shock would break her ribs. I recoiled at the thought, yet breathed a sigh of relief. Extreme measures to keep her alive in her present torment were so wrong and cruel.

I found a nurse, introduced myself and started asking questions. I expressed my anguish at the excessive treatments when Esther should be in hospice. She nodded in agreement and with tears in her eyes said, "I'm sorry, but Esther's husband has legal papers which blocks your access to all her medical information. You'll have to get all reports from him personally." I looked at her in shock and could no longer contain my tears. Like a white flag of truce, she pushed a box of tissues toward me, took me by the arm and ushered me to an empty consult room. She hugged me before she left and said, "Take as long as you need."

I needed to see my girl! I blew my nose and stemmed the flow thinking, *I can cry later.*

I entered the cramped ER cubicle where Esther lay. Wide pleading eyes met mine and I'd never felt so inept as a mom. Her inability to speak, left me awash with sorrow and frustration. Amidst my inner tumble of snarled questions I wondered what *her* true desires were. Romeo sat to her right making it impossible to at least ask her some yes and no questions. To me, the expression in her eyes had the look of trapped prey. I noticed sores at the corner of her mouth and thought, *oh no, all she needs are cold sores added to her pain.*

Later I found out the medical team had dug seven Dilaudid pills (strong opioid pain meds) from between her cheek and gums. Her well-meaning, but untrained caretakers didn't know she could no longer swallow. So the pills collected there. I cringed to think of what her mouth may have looked like inside if the blisters on the outside were indicative. No wonder she couldn't talk.

I sat to her left and the only thing I knew would bring her comfort was to sing worship songs. Sometimes the grief is so deep all one can do is say, "Jesus."

The Bill Gaither song, "There's Just Something About That Name," came to mind.

Jesus, Jesus, Jesus

There's just something about that name

Master, Savior, Jesus,

like the sunshine after the rain

Jesus, Jesus, Jesus

Let all heaven and earth proclaim,

Kings and kingdoms shall all pass away,

But there's something about that name.

As I sang softly, Romeo became agitated and said it was disturbing Esther. I looked at her peaceful face and said, "Look at her, she's calm and serene. Praise songs soothe her."

I continued.

He left.

☺☺☺

A memory flashed of my former vision where evil army planes swarmed Seth, Esther and me. As I remembered, the wall of heavenly warrriors appeared before me again, but it had changed. Instead of a solid wall, there were holes in it. *Oh no! Was it disintegrating?*

I sat transfixed as a fully armed warrior charged from the wall with his sword in attack position. I realized the wall wasn't falling apart, but the gaps represented those fighting on our behalf. On the tailwind of this scene the Spirit revealed another truth. When the army of planes had flown over us in my original vision, the pilots leared and threatened, but never touched us.

It reminded me Satan's weapons were intimidation, lies, and fear. He had no authority or power stronger than the death and resurrection of Jesus. Esther was dying, yet she was safe as we all were. Our eternal souls were held in our Savior's hands. The updated vision gave me hope and strength. Even if it *felt* like God was absent, He was not only present, but fighting *for* us.

REFLECT

There are many heartbreaking cancer stories, but do you see the invisible hand-to-hand spiritual combat as you read Esther's story? Have you realized we're in a war on this earth? Do you recognize the unseen spiritual war surrounding you too?

APPLY

We walk in a physical world with invisible waves all around us and think nothing of it. We live with television and cell phone rays; radio, Wi-Fi and satellite signals. Physically we can't taste, smell, see, touch, or hear them, yet we know they're real. We don't think these invisible connections are magic or even know how they work; we just accept them and do life.

Just because we can't perceive the unseen war of demons and angels doesn't mean they don't exist.

Check out these two excellent articles by Max Anders:

1. "How Much do you Know About the Invisible World?"
2. "Three Steps to Winning Your Spiritual War"

https://www.maxanders.com/how-much-do-you-know-about-the-invisible-world/

PRAYER

Dear Heavenly Father, It's so helpful to understand there is an invisible war occurring right here on earth in my life. As I study your Word which I understand is a spiritual book, and address these issues, open my spiritual eyes. Help me to comprehend how to stand firm in my faith recognizing Jesus already won the war. Jesus *is* my armor. Make me ever mindful to bathe my mind in your Word and utilize it as my sword.

Chapter 42

Signs of Love

Postures erect, and hands poised with fingers intertwined, nine sixth-graders waited for their teacher to start the music. With the first notes, arms and hands raised artistically to speak words without human voice. Sign Language is an elegant form of communication, especially when put to a melody.

The director and sixth grade teacher, a petite young woman, appeared more schoolgirl than adult. An Interpreter of American Sign Language, she insisted on performance perfection. She went on to be a full time ASL Interpreter and teacher for many years in a local high school, but the students from her first year of teaching were etched on her heart forever. Esther held a special place as one of those students.

Twenty years later, married with a daughter of her own, she played a significant role during the last days of Esther's life. Over the years we'd stayed connected through piano lessons, ballet, and our mutual faith. When

Esther's cancer returned, she stepped up with meals, prayers, and hands-on help.

This was especially meaningful as medical updates were kept from us by Romeo's legal action when Esther entered the hospital for the last ten days of her life in July 2016. Focused more on Esther's welfare and realizing her time was short, we didn't get entangled in a legal battle, but God provided an alternate route of communication. He made a way where none seemed possible.

My heart bows in worship as I reflect on the Lord's provision and perfect timing of events during her last days.

With hesitant pace, a diminutive lady made her way down the long hospital corridor. Dark hair piled high, skilled make-up application, and fashionable attire were her earmarks. The one thing missing—her usual jaunty step.

The thought of seeing her healthy young student so close to death would test her own faith. I'm sure having her own teenage daughter made this event even more difficult. The mind leaps—*what if?* A prayer warrior with a tender heart, her visit was a brave act of kindness and support.

During her visit, like the pieces of a puzzle coming together, her face lit up as she realized, *this is the hospital where my husband did his clinicals while earning his nursing degree.*

She returned to the hospital early the next day with her husband at her side. Seth and I joined them and made our way to Esther's room. Not only was this the hospital he'd worked in, but he soon realized he'd been assigned to the same floor. Many of the previous staff were still there. What are the chances?!

I'm reminded of the story in Matthew 8:23-27 where Jesus rebuked the storm threatening to drown the disciples in their boat, but at His rebuke, the waters became completely calm. They asked, "What kind of man is this? Even the winds and waves obey him!" We witnessed such a miracle as God provided a medical professional who accessed updates on Esther's condition and relayed them to us. Our hearts *became completely calm.*

As I write this, I'm still amazed at God's consistent, purposeful presence and how He took crushing waves of contentious evil and transformed them into ripples of peace.

And my God shall supply all your need according to His riches in glory by Christ Jesus. Philippians 4:19NKJ

~ Her teacher would grace us with another cherished gift
in the near future ~

REFLECT
Have you ever been in a situation where black dense hopelessness brought you to the brink of despair?

APPLY
The word despair translates as hopelessness and destroys courage which stops all effort.

Desperation, which is an active state of despair, produces a furious struggle against adverse circumstances. Use this desperation-type-energy to focus on the source of your true strength.

I can do all things through Christ who strengthens me.
Philippians 4:13 NKJV

The power of fear is focus. The power of faith is focus. You choose.

PRAYER
Dear Heavenly Father,
As I cry out to you over and over again in desperation-type energy, I know I can trust you even when You seem silent and I don't understand. You are aware of my circumstances and supply exactly what I need. Never too early. Never too late.

Chapter 43

Do You Believe in Heaven?

Medical staff predicted Esther wouldn't make it through the last week of July. To avoid our long commute, a friend rented a hotel room for us so we could stay near the hospital. One morning during the same week, my sister, Katrina, had a vision of Jesus standing with arms outstretched ready to receive our sweet girl.

I felt Esther's time of departure was near as Romeo and I stood at the head of Esther's bed, one on each side. Quietly, I whispered in her ear, "Esther, it's alright to go; Jesus is waiting for you." I urged Romeo to speak words of release to her and tell her he would be okay. I felt she needed to hear that.

Late afternoon, former members of Esther and Romeo's Bible study group from their church gathered in her hospital room. I noticed a young woman who stood next to Esther's bed. She spoke sweetly to her and stroked her hand. She introduced herself as Amberlynn. Her sweetness permeated the room with Jesus' presence. It felt like another God-hug just when I needed it most.

Then the pastor who had led her baptism arrived. He entered, bringing his compassionate presence, and spoke words of comfort from relevant scriptures like: Romans 8 where Paul states that *nothing* can separate us from the love of God because of Jesus' life, death, and resurrection. Not death, angels, demons, or anything in all creation. Also, I Corinthians 15 where Paul writes, "Death has been swallowed up in victory." And in John 11 at the tomb of Lazarus when Jesus said: "I am the resurrection and the life. The one who believes in me will live, even though they die;" he then closed with prayer.

Soft strains of melody drifted over the scene as Seth quietly led us in Amazing Grace. Although difficult to sing with all the emotion of the moment, the words encouraged us. Romeo made a hasty retreat from the room when the singing started. The small Bible study group spoke kind words of support and left a short time later.

Romeo returned, walked to the far side of the room near the windows and tilted forward, his head pressed against the wall. He seemed to be in the throes of a decision. I expected him to speak words of release to Esther. He then turned and walked to the side of her bed facing me. Like a veil, I saw a shadow drop over his countenance. He became angry and accused Seth and me of summoning the pastor without his knowledge.

I should have been prepared for accusations from Romeo by now, but they were so unexpected and illogical I could never quite believe what I was hearing. I tried to explain we had nothing to do with it. He then insisted we should leave; he wanted to be alone with Esther for the night. Seth and I, aghast at the thought of leaving her side with the end so near, were struck dumb as we attempted to digest his words.

After a tense pause, Seth responded, "I promised Esther I'd be with her to the end, and I can't deny her that now." Seth refused to leave. Torn over the possibility of ugly altercations, I vacillated. I felt a dark spirit had been let loose as Heidi's husband entered the fray along with Jack and Candy. Amidst threats to call security to have Seth thrown out, I thought it would turn physical. The din of voices escalated. Everyone shouted an opinion.

I'd had enough, and very uncharacteristically I screamed, "SHUT UP! You have no right to speak into this! You're *not* family! Please leave!"

Candy spoke up and said, "she's right." She and Jack left. Heidi's husband stayed.

Heated, loud discussion continued, and I begged Seth to leave. Hospital personnel were becoming alarmed at the intensity of the conflict. Landing in jail would gain nothing. Since we had a hotel room close by, I pleaded for Seth to go with me. A reluctant agreement was made for us to come back after Romeo had a couple of hours alone with Esther. We spent a restless night waiting for a call that never came. From there, things plunged into further chaos as we walked out our personal Via Dolorosa.

To watch her unnecessary suffering was more than I could endure.

The e-mail I wrote on July 25th gives insight into that pain:

The strife between friends and family members has been great as one side wants her to live as long as possible, withholding pain meds to keep her awake to hear the prayers for her healing. The merciful pray in silence the Lord will take her quickly to stop the torture and suffering, but are kept at bay and not allowed to speak last words of love and comfort.

We have no official authority to act on her behalf, so personally I can't watch the mutilation and torture of my beloved Esther any longer. The thought of being away from her side as she dies is torture beyond bearing, and makes me feel like the most wicked mother! But to save my own sanity, physical, spiritual, and emotional health I've had to leave.

Our enemies tear at our hearts and reputations with unbelievable slander as we are crushed over and over again. Former friends as well as strangers seem to believe the vicious lies and stand in unrighteous judgement. They gather in clusters around the hospital, whisper and stare, until we feel like lepers and vermin deserving to be cast out. It's like observing an evil spirit drop a film over their eyes, putting them under a spell. Esther seems to be a type of Christ that demons spill their malicious destructive hatred on.

Please be on your faces before the Lord on our behalf, praying for us in this hour of unprecedented torment. We know this battle is spiritual and not just about what is seen.

I have a whole new view of what my heavenly Father went through as he watched His beloved, innocent Son be tortured and put to death in the cruelest way. He knows our pain and is aware of our circumstances.

I'm so thankful the Lord has laid a foundation in our lives of knowing our true identity in Christ which helps us stand in these evil times.

With Love, Grace and Warrior Hearts we Stand!"

Esther's Marmie

REFLECT

Jesus states, *In this world you will have trouble. But take heart! I have overcome the world.* John 16:33b

What does *your* response reveal as you walk out your personal heartaches? When you don't genuinely believe in life after death, you will cling tenaciously to this life, even to the detriment of those you claim to love.

What we really believe is revealed through our actions. If we believe in heaven, even when we're attacked, the hurt may be extreme, but it doesn't decimate us.

APPLY

If it's your desire, would you embrace with your heart the following words and pray them aloud and then share your decision with another person.

PRAYER

Lord, I realize now that my whole life has been a search for heaven on earth. I long to know, to taste, to feel the truth that is true, the love that is genuine, the Master who will never let me down. You died for me so many years ago on a painful cross, and I realize now that You took the payment for all my sins—every one of them. How I long to be relieved of their burden! Just as You rose from the dead, conquering death forever, I choose right now to accept eternal life—to know that death will

have no hold on me. And I will pursue You down that path toward the Eternal City with every breath I breathe for the rest of this life until the day You and I meet face to face. Amen

(Salvation Prayer – 31 Days to Happiness by David Jeremiah)

Chapter 44

Dress Rehearsal

Since the altercation, I'd taken a couple of days to renew, seek counsel, and pray. I realized I couldn't stay away from my dear girl no matter what the cost.

I stepped out of the hospital elevator and Esther's friend, Vera, stood waiting to enter. All aflutter she blurted, "A lady just saw Esther in the hospital halls dancing in a white dress!"

Vera, wasn't making sense. Esther lay in a coma.

"What are you talking about? That's impossible."

"But she saw her!"

"Who saw her?"

"A patient named Kimberly across the hall from Esther's room. Go talk to her. I'm running late for an appointment," Vera said, as the elevator doors slid closed.

Mystified, I stepped into the restroom and glanced at my pale reflection in the mirror. I hardly recognized the woman staring back at me. My usual neat bob clung damp and limp—emphasizing hollow, sad eyes. I splashed cool water on my face. Atlanta's July humidity added weight to my weariness as I trudged the familiar route to my daughter's hospital room. I hoped Romeo wouldn't be there.

Esther's last ten days were one nightmare after another. Each evening, medical staff predicted she would not survive. Romeo continued to refuse hospice. He controlled her care and withheld pain meds to comply with Cecelia's desire to keep her awake so she could hear her prayers. I agonized as I watched Esther's unnecessary suffering. I'd think, *it cannot get any more gruesome,* but it did.

Then—something phenomenal happened. As I continued down the hall to Esther's bedside, my thoughts returned to Vera's words *...dancing...white dress,* they rang true. Esther loved to dance. We knew death inched near, and according to Revelation 19 she would soon be wearing white.

And to her was granted that she should be
arrayed in fine linen, clean and white:
for the fine linen is the righteousness of saints.
Revelation 19:8 KJV

Like the discovery of a subterranean cavern full of precious gems, a sense God was up to something extraordinary began to lift my spirit.

As I approached Esther's room, a lady with a sweet smile stepped out from the room across the hall.

"Are you Kimberly?" I asked.

"No, Kimberly's my daughter."

"I'm Esther's mother. I've heard she had an unusual experience which involved Esther.

Do you think she'd be willing to talk to me?"

"Yes, please come in. I know she would love to meet you. The event has left her quite shaken, but I'll let her explain."

I entered the low-lit room and introduced myself. Kimberly seemed a bit shy but warmed quickly when she understood Esther was my daughter.

"How do you know Esther?" I asked quietly.

"I don't, and that's what's so crazy. I've never even seen her before," Kimberly replied. "I spoke to her friend earlier... *Umm,* Heidi. I think?"

"Oh," I said, "Yes, Heidi has been helping her this week."

"My Mom had seen Heidi come in and out of Esther's room and overheard a nurse comment she'd been helping her friend. I've had two near-death-experiences (NDE's) in the last week where I had seen a young woman I didn't recognize. I've wondered if Heidi's friend might be her. My mom had Heidi come talk to me. When I told Heidi about my experience and the young woman I'd seen, she took out her cell phone and showed me Esther's picture. She was the one—your daughter, Esther!"

Kimberly continued, "The sense I'd entered the Twilight Zone or gone insane frightened me and I burst into tears. It's a wonder they didn't have to resuscitate me again! Nothing has *ever* happened to me like that before."

As I continued to question, I found Kimberly lived fifty miles away and asked, "How did you end up at *this* hospital?"

I stood in awe as Kimberly shared her story.

"I passed out at work, and they brought me to the closest hospital. I'd never fainted before and had no clue I had a rare blood disorder called TTP. It's where the blood doesn't get enough oxygen and vital organs shut down. The ER doctor's friend, also a physician, had just written a book on TTP. What a coincidence, right?"

She continued, "While in the ER my heart stopped and I had to be resuscitated. During that time, I had an experience where I left my body and hovered over the medical team working on me. The ER crew stabilized me and after some further testing, I went home with an appointment to return four days later for minor surgery. After the procedure I spent the night in the hospital, but during the early morning hours I hemorrhaged and flat-lined again. I experienced another NDE."

(I thought it interesting this occurred the same day our rights were terminated when Esther re-entered the hospital for the last time.)

Kimberly explained her NDE, "A scene opened like a window into another world, where a girl with long dark hair hovered above her own dying form on the bed. Pointing down, she repeated over and over, *'That's not me —this is me!'* as she pointed to herself. Although no words were spoken between us, I knew it was important for others to know. Then the window closed."

Kimberly continued, "Then another scene opened and the same girl stood in front of a floor-length mirror admiring her beautiful white dress as she twirled and danced. I couldn't see anyone, but I sensed another presence in the room. The girl glanced to her right as if speaking to someone, then whirled around and gasped, 'Oh! They can see me?' Immediately the window closed.

The third time, no longer in her hospital room, she stood in front of the mirror again in an open white space. Here, I saw her playful vibrant spirit. She was laughing as she flipped her hair from side to side trying out different hairstyles. I watched her joyful antics until once again the window shut and didn't reopen."

Kimberly paused, looked at me with a slight shiver and said, "I know it sounds crazy, but it was your daughter I saw."

Like a beautiful God-woven tapestry of lives and circumstances—Kimberly's story revitalized my heart. I knew in some inexplicable way God held our girl in a special place.

Over the next months and even years now, each of those scenes have brought tears, laughter, and peace to this Momma's broken heart. When Satan, the author of lies, taunts me with the ugly scenes of her dying form, I know she's dancing with the Prince of Peace. I see the glory of her hair restored. I hear the echo of her voice: *"Marmie, that's not me, this is me!"*

REFLECT

*Dear brothers and sisters, when troubles of any kind come your way, consider it an **opportunity** for great joy.* James 1:2 NLT (emphasis mine)

These words in James seem ridiculous when we're in the middle of the battle, right? But James says to **consider**: to think carefully about, examine, appraise, review, study, and ponder.

Now, in hindsight when I stop and reflect, I realize I did experience *joy and I did grow in endurance.* Yes, a thousand times yes.

Before Kimberly entered the scene, the darkness felt overwhelming. Then her visions into the unseen world spoke life into me. Instead of a nervous breakdown, I experienced a celebration of life and heaven and Jesus' resurrection power. Have *you* ever experienced moments of encouragement during a time of grief?

APPLY

James says there's an *opportunity* for joy which suggests you may need to search, ponder, consider and then *choose* to embrace it. Sometimes, joy or miracles may not be something we pursue. It's more like we trip over them as we run our race of faith. Miracles can reignite our faith, even start our faith, but they can't sustain it. We need a steady diet of God's Word and a practiced sensitivity to follow the direction of His Spirit.

PRAYER

Dear Heavenly Father,

Help me to choose faith in your goodness, right in the middle of my heartbreak. Reveal your grace and beauty in it so I will experience joy.

Chapter 45

Hospital Anguish

The crescendo of trauma during Esther's last three days became deafening. Like drums on a battlefield beating a relentless cadence, my heart quaked from the pounding. A spiritual war between good and evil erupted like nothing I'd ever experienced—executed with stealth and deception. Psychiatric professionals state verbal abuse is worse than physical assaults. It's unseen and doesn't leave visible wounds. Such were the emotional lacerations on my heart.

As I peered into Esther's hospital room, I jolted. There stood Susan, a former friend of Esther's giving orders like she was in charge. Due to life circumstances, she and Esther's friendship had waned and become distant. So now, it seemed odd for her to be directing Esther's care. Months earlier she'd aligned herself with Romeo and I assumed this was the reason for her cool demeanor toward Seth and me. That, mixed with Romeo's lies, had drawn a thick line between us.

I remained at the entrance and watched another young woman I didn't recognize stroke Esther's arm. The connection of touch is powerful. Both parties are comforted. Watching someone suffer creates a desire to reach out and soothe their pain away. As this stranger comforted Esther, Susan stood on the other side of the bed adjusting pillows and sheets.

I stepped back into the hall to regain my composure. The unknown girl soon left and I walked to Esther's bedside where she lay cocooned in her coma. I reached out, needing the connection of touch myself, and lightly stroked her arm.

Like a slap in the face, Susan reprimanded me. "Please don't do that! Her skin is so thin and dry now." I lashed back: "I just watched a stranger rubbing her arm and you said nothing! And you tell *me,* her *mother,* I'm not allowed to touch her?" My aberrant retort stopped her. The stinging insult caused my heart to contract and it felt like its rhythms would cease. If ever my daughter needed my touch, it was now.

To love this daughter with every cell of my body and be set aside as someone to be dismissed…well, there were no words to express the humiliation of such judgement.

To be treated dismissively *and* blocked from speaking to medical personnel about her condition was a dishonor beyond belief.

Later, when Seth arrived at the hospital, Romeo said to a friend, "Hurry and grab the chair next to Esther before Seth gets it." The day became a cat and mouse game of chair snatching and blatant cruel remarks, implying Seth and me as vile parents.

The sheet over Esther became twisted and exposed a portion of her leg. Romeo reached over and covered her. "Esther wouldn't like that," he commented, followed by a snide glance at Seth and me. The intention of his message to support his lies—yet even now I can hardly wrap my mind around the vicious subterfuge.

This day of shockwaves had just begun. Esther, still attached to an I.V. drip, required several changes of her gowns and bedding throughout the day. Her swollen body prevented use of a catheter to drain her urine, so liquids were excreted unchecked.

Susan announced "It's time to change the bedding and I need everyone to leave the room."

After our earlier face-off, Susan's demeanor toward me was kinder and she invited me to stay and help. I gasped and recoiled as Esther cried out when they rolled her over on the side where the tumor had grown into her sciatic nerve. To me, Susan seemed insensitive and rough. My thoughts raged; *do they even understand where her tumor is? Why is Susan not more compassionate and tender with how she handles her?* Even in her comatose state, Esther moaned loud as her gown was removed and sheets pulled from under her.

To watch her unnecessary agony unhinged me. Right then I decided not to put myself through this process again.

The IV's *should* be stopped.

She *should* be in hospice care.

She *should* be kept comfortable and out of pain.

We *should* be able to say our goodbyes.

I knew I was right—but powerless.

The staggering nightmare continued...

When time came for the next change of Esther's bedclothes, Seth begged me to stay in the room with her so I could save a chair beside Esther. With *extreme* reluctance I stayed.

Sliding a fresh case onto a pillow, I watched and cringed as Esther was rolled onto her side again. My wail accompanied her cry of pain as a different scene turned my world into horror. Her exposed back which had been flesh-colored before had turned blue-grey, and now indentations like slashes covered the surface. She looked like a living corpse, preyed upon by demonic forces. The howl of my grief erupted unbidden and unstoppable. I ran into the hall. Others came running, including Romeo. They thought she had died.

I thought, *you people don't get it! Compared to this needless torture, death for her would be a victory.* The now, familiar verses flowed through my mind:

The righteous perish, and no one takes it to heart;

the devout are taken away, and no one understands

that the righteous are taken away to be spared from evil.

Those who walk uprightly enter into peace; they find rest

as they lie in death.

Isaiah 57:1-2

REFLECT

Several months earlier, seeking levity where ever we could find it, Esther and I reflected on the *why* of her journey back into cancer. Our recent impactful study of the book of Esther triggered Esther's response. "Well Marmie, the book of Esther *is* right next to Job in the Bible!" We laughed at the irony.

If there ever existed a man who deserved to lament, Job of the Bible did. I'm not saying our trials compared to what he went through, but there *were* a lot of similarities.

- Satan himself challenged God to test Job, a righteous devout man.
- My vision of the army of planes suggested a divine awareness of what was coming. Esther loved God with her whole heart, and lived out a righteous life. I wonder if something similar took place regarding Esther at God's throne?

- Yes, Job lost ten children in a wind storm.
- Esther lost *all* of her ability to bear a child.

- Job's friends started out well by encouraging him with their presence. Then made the mistake of opening their mouths with all their opinions.

- Esther's friends started out well with all their prayers and support, but many made the same mistake offering opinions and solutions which added to her misery.

- Job, the wealthiest man in the East lost all material possessions.
- Esther's cancer and other factors caused loss of all material riches.

APPLY

So, the question has to be asked: *Why was Job restored and Esther not?* As I contemplated, I realized both Job and Esther *were* restored, just in different ways. I think she got the better deal.

PRAYER

Dear Heavenly Father

When everything and everyone around me is asking, "how can a good God allow such pain and agony?" You God, already answered the question when you allowed *your* Son, Jesus, to be brutalized by the most horrendous torture ever perpetrated in order to provide a heavenly home where we'll never suffer again.

Chapter 46

Fighting for Esther

Each day splintered into multiple battle fronts. Returning to the hospital the next day, we watched again as pain meds were withheld and Esther's groaning found us speaking our distress into the melee.

Since according to Romeo, no plans had been made for Esther's funeral, Seth and I had bought two gravesites. Regardless of what Romeo had in mind, we planned our own memorial service where we could celebrate her in peace with our family and friends who'd been our prayer warriors and hands-on support.

Word had spread among hospital staff two funerals were being considered. Seth and I were summoned to meet with Romeo and the hospital's social worker. Seth wouldn't leave Esther's side so Esther's nurse friend, volunteered to go with me. As we entered the consultation room, I staggered at the sight of Jack sitting next to Romeo. A chill clinched at my stomach as my heart rhythms increased. A woman I assumed to be the counselor waited with them.

Esther's medical friend and I took a seat. Romeo insisted she leave. I vacillated. A natural peace maker, my desire for reconciliation and harmony created a false expectation. My foggy brain forgot I dealt with someone bent on deception and malice. To relieve stress, I agreed for her to go. I've asked myself "Why?" a hundred times since. *Why* didn't I insist Jack—who had ignored Esther's pain and berated her and later myself with his sermonizing—leave as well or refuse to dismiss her friend? It's so obvious in hindsight.

The social worker opened, "I understand there are two funerals being planned."

Dryly I commented, "That's news to me. As of yesterday, nothing had been arranged."

Romeo proceeded to spin off layers of lies as he said, "Two friends are on-line searching for an urn right now. Yesterday, Esther and I had a discussion and we agreed on cremation."

I fired back, "Esther was in a coma and such a conversation would have been impossible. Regardless, I know her. She would have been appalled at the thought of cremation."

Romeo mumbled, "Well, maybe it was a few days ago, but it doesn't matter."

The contentious conversation vacillated between Romeo's lies and Jack's dismissive hand waves and comments. The counselor made suggestions and tried to bring some sanity to the situation. I left to get Seth's input. After I recounted the combative discourse with Seth, we agreed to hand over all the planning of the funeral to Romeo. As her husband, he should be dealing with this anyway. We'd only stepped in because no preparations had been made. We still planned on our own service later.

After the shattering, emotional, hang-on-by-a-fingernail day, I had just burrowed under my blanket that evening when a blasphemous thought impaled my gauzy-shrouded brain. *What if Romeo asked Jack to give the sermon at the funeral?!* The thought sickened me. How dishonoring to Esther. She would hate it. I reached for my cell phone and sent a text to Romeo and asked him to meet me in the hospital consultation room the next day. We'd given Romeo carte blanche without one request for anything; he'd surely honor this one request.

Romeo and I met. The tension in the room felt volatile. With a deep breath, and a prayer for a calm heart, I asked him to share what he had planned for the service, my focus on *who* would give the eulogies and sermon. He said, "Probably Pastor John." The pastor of the church where Esther grew up. I breathed a sigh of relief.

"I only have one request and here's why." I told him the story of Jack and Candy's trip to the doctor with Esther and her request to never let them near her again. "I only ask you honor Esther by not allowing them to have a part in the service." He said nothing as his lips tightened into a straight line.

I sighed and thought, *I've done what I could.*

Unaware, I had just given Romeo the ammunition to wound us again.

☮☮☮

The next day sitting outside Esther's hospital room, Seth and I had reached the limit of our tolerance. We could no longer sit on the sidelines and watch Esther's *avoidable* torment.

During a moment of brain clarity, Seth commented: "I remember her oncologist promised he would *not* allow Esther to suffer." We then realized, he thought she was in hospice care. He'd not seen her since she'd been readmitted to the hospital.

A steely resolve gripped us as we left the hospital and marched across the road to his office. A place so familiar, we didn't stop at the desk but maintained a determined pace down the hall to his office. He stood just outside and recognized us immediately. Concern etched his face at our surprise interruption. Our pained voices painted the picture of what was taking place as we ended with… "You promised you wouldn't allow her to suffer like this!"

The doctor stated firmly, "I'll take care of it."

Later, Romeo raged at Seth over the phone regarding our interference. Doctor Zak had visited and upped Esther's pain medication. A surprise visit by an ambulance in the evening swept Esther away to the nearest hospice facility. If we'd known the doctor had the power to act on her behalf, we would have requested his help long before.

Early Wednesday morning, July 31, 2016, we visited Esther. Her relaxed pain-free countenance brought me comfort even though I knew the end loomed near. I had questions, so proceeded to the front desk and spoke with the nurse.

"Since you work with the dying on a regular basis, can you give me some idea of how long my daughter has left?"

She asked, "How long since she's been able to eat and drink?"

I calculated for a moment and said, "Ten days."

"It's rare for them to last longer than that."

Curious, I asked, "When she cried out in pain the last few days, I was told she couldn't feel anything, because she was in a coma. Is that true?"

Her head jerked back as she looked at me like I'd asked the most foolish question. "If she so much as grimaces, she feels pain."

"I knew it!" Esther had suffered unreasonable torture to gratify the selfish need of Romeo to hang on to her as long as possible and her so-called *friends* supported him. Unbelievable!

Visitors started drifting in, and to my surprise, many were from Esther's former place of employment. The office building located within a half mile of the hospice facility made it convenient for co-workers to visit and say final good byes. By the end of the day, everyone she'd worked with had come to see her. All except *one*, even though prodded by other employees to come and ask forgiveness for the way he'd treated her. Yes, the cruel bigoted manager. Rather than anger, I only felt pity for someone filled with such bias and malice. A shriveled soul.

Just when I thought we'd found a place of peace where we could find some closure, the ultimate battle launched.

REFLECT

Have you ever fought for someone who couldn't fight for themselves? A loved one? A friend? A neighbor? Maybe you couldn't have lived with yourself if you hadn't stood up for them.

APPLY

> *Speak up for those who cannot speak for themselves;*
> *Ensure justice for those being crushed.*
> *Yes, speak up for the poor and helpless,*
> *And see that they get justice.*
> Proverbs 31:8-9 NLT

PRAYER

Dear Heavenly Father,

Help me to remember when I refuse to help those who are being mistreated in my sphere of influence, I'm refusing to help you.

Chapter 47

Falsely Accused

Vera visited the day Esther entered hospice care and asked to meet privately with Seth and me. Seth refused. He didn't trust her for two reasons—a recent hostile rant toward him at the hospital and her prior false prophecy about Esther's baptism.

The past two weeks Vera had seemed off-kilter. Even Romeo commented on her erratic behavior. There was no question of her past loyalty and love for Esther; but in hindsight, I believe a hyper-desperation for Esther to live came from her own recent loss of two core relationships. One led to a nervous breakdown the previous summer and the other, a second-time breakup with her finance' brought immense rejection and heartache. I don't think she realized the undercurrent of those emotional wounds in her desire to save Esther.

Further compromised by her current two week fast, Vera's judgement became skewed, even allowing the enemy to breach her former knowledge of our family. Like a drowning person grasping at a toothpick for survival, a twisted perspective resulted.

A long day left me emotionally weary but hungry. I left Esther's hospice room to meet Seth at the car to go find a quick meal. Vera caught me near the exit and pleaded for me to talk with her. Over the years, she'd been a supportive friend. How could I refuse. (I wasn't aware of her prior verbal attack on Seth.) For privacy we stepped into the small hospice chapel where she took a chair facing me.

Tears brimmed as she struggled to speak. "I can't tell you how hard this is for me, but I've been desperate to share a new revelation with you. You can still save Esther."

I knew Vera had aligned herself more with Romeo from my previous encounter at Esther's home two weeks before. But sometimes it became difficult to keep all the mental chess pieces of this nightmare straight. In my mind she knew us, she had stayed away from Romeo for seven months after he'd terrified her the previous summer. After that altercation, she even accused Romeo of having an evil spirit. I never expected her to be completely taken in by his lies.

Vera began "You told me Seth had been abused as a child and we know abused people abuse others."

My mouth gaped as I realized where she was going. I remembered our conversation the previous February before Esther's baptism when we discussed our family background. She'd probed to see if something in *us* held back God's healing from Esther. I'd explained some of our past, not realizing she'd jumped to false conclusions and twist what I had told her. She inferred someone in our family had done something reprehensible to Esther, and Esther was now paying for our sin. Vera concluded—only we had the power to save her.

I thrust my opened palm toward her. "Stop! You're basing what you think on a false memory or confusion about what I said."

"Don't lie to me!" Her accusing voice volleyed back.

I recoiled. The verbal blow landed hard. "I distinctly remember our conversation, Vera, and if that's what you believe, you misunderstood."

Then, like the wheels of a semi-truck crushing a wounded puppy into the pavement, her words decimated my fragile heart.

"A mother knows when abuse is occurring to her child and you let it happen. *Your* guilt is worse! If you'll go and ask Esther's forgiveness right now, she'll be healed."

"You're wrong, Vera. *Nothing* like that happened."

"You're going to sit there and lie to me?" she snapped and flung her last lasered zinger. "It's all going to come out. There are witnesses."

I sat stunned and speechless for a moment as I tried to process what she meant.

"What? Who are you talking about?"

She shook her head, "I can't say."

For several months Romeo had made furtive comments to us, such as "Your hypocrisy is going to be revealed and the masks will come off. You're going to be exposed."

Emotionally beaten to the ground, fear and doubt crept a stealthy path into my thoughts. For the first time I questioned... *Could I have missed something? Or... does Romeo have someone in the wings prepared to give false testimony? Would he use her memorial service as his platform?* In psychological warfare, I knew an enemy accuses a victim of the very thing they themselves are guilty of. It's called gas lighting, and it's crazy-making. Could that be going on here?

I left the room so shaken I could hardly walk. I went to Esther's bedside. My fingers trembled as I stroked her arm. I leaned down, kissed her cheek and whispered in her ear, "I love you my sweet girl," then retrieved my purse and left. The enemy had done his cruelest work. Divide and conquer with fear, lies, and deception.

Seth waited in the car, wondering where I'd disappeared to. As I neared the car, my legs became like broken hinges. My knees buckled as I reached for the door handle and almost collapsed on the sidewalk. In shock, I tumbled into the car seat unable to speak.

Irritated, Seth asked, "Where have you been?" My silence and grief-stricken face must have frightened him. His eyes widened. "Is she gone?"

I shook my head.

"What's wrong then?"

I tried to speak, but no words came as my breath seemed to evaporate. Gasping for air, I stuttered "I..." gulping, I could only choke out lone syllables, "She..." silence as I tried to suck in air.

"You're scaring me, what's going on?" he insisted.

"Vera..."

"Honey, surely you didn't let her get to you?"

My mouth opened and closed dumbly and I felt like a fish gasping for life on a muddy river bank. Still trying to calm down enough to get out an intelligible sentence I continued to stutter lone syllables as choking sobs began.

It seemed an eternity, but probably only minutes before I could explain what happened.

We discussed the possibilities of what Romeo might have in store for us and the possible legal implications. We knew we needed help. I called my dear friend and professional counselor who had made herself available 24-7. We drove to her house 90 minutes away. Appetite gone. Dinner forgotten.

Much later, after wise counsel and a conversation with our pastor, we collapsed into bed. The red L.E.D. lights on the nightstand clock displayed the early hour... 4:30 a.m.

Up at 7 a.m. and anxious to get to Esther, Seth glanced at his phone and saw a text from Romeo. Esther had passed at 4:29 a.m. His text explained we only had two hours after the time of death to see her before they took her away. It had already been 2 ½ hours.

Our phones had been on all night. If he'd just called rather than sent a text we would have heard and answered. Separated by 50 miles in morning traffic, we didn't have a chance —*even* if they waited. Hoping to see her at the morgue before cremation, we contacted the hospice staff.

They had been given instructions, "Do *not* tell her parents where she's been taken."

Long ago we'd quit saying, "Surely, this can't get any worse!"

REFLECT

Have there been times in your life when grief seemed to have no end? Yet, even the idea of comfort enraged you because the removal of your anguish would diminish the *value* of what had been taken? Do you feel like no one else has ever suffered like you?

APPLY

The prophet Habakkuk laments the evil surrounding him and may also reflect your own pain.

> *"GOD, how long do I have to cry out for help*
> *before you listen?*
> *How many times do I have to yell,*
> *'Help! Murder! Police!'*
> *before you come to the rescue?*
> *Why do you force me to look at evil,*
> *stare trouble in the face day after day?"*
> Habakkuk 1:2-3 (The Message)

An important dialogue continues as Habakkuk questions God's goodness amidst so much injustice, evil, and tragedy in his world. Sound familiar? Yes, to me also. Then Habakkuk concludes his honest discourse and requests God to *remember mercy*. When he examines the big picture, this short book of the Bible ends in an amazing declaration of faith. Basically, he states:

Even though everything fails, I will rejoice in the Lord and be joyful.

* Read through the three short chapters of Habakkuk.
* Google Chuck Swindoll's overview on Habakkuk to help you see God's end purpose.

PRAYER

Dear Father, I feel no one else has ever gone through the depth of sorrow I'm experiencing, but when I read Habakkuk who lived hundreds of years ago expressing the same throes of grief, I know that's not true. Lord, enlighten my mind and comfort my heart with your truth, so I can say with Habakkuk:

Though the fig tree does not bud and there are no grapes on the vines,

Though the olive crop fails and the fields produce no food,

Though there are no sheep in the pen and no cattle in the stalls,

Yet I will rejoice in the LORD, I will be joyful in God my Savior.

The Sovereign LORD is my strength; he makes my feet like the feet of a deer,

he enables me to tread on the heights.

Habakkuk 3:17-19

Chapter 48

A Funeral or a Flogging?

When Seth read the text from Romeo, I realized Esther had slipped away to her heavenly home about the time we fell asleep. Like a resurrection, my hands lifted toward the heavens. I could not grieve. My heart felt only joy and relief as I repeated over and over, "Thank you Lord Jesus, she's with You. She's free! No more pain or heartache." For thirty minutes, I walked through the house with arms raised, praising God. She was home! Safe! Words from Isaiah 57 drifted and soothed....*the righteous are taken away to be spared from evil. Those who walk uprightly enter into peace; they find rest as they lie in death.*

A knock on the door announced our pastor's arrival. The polar opposites of relief and sorrow collided. Our present separation from Esther became reality as I fell into his arms and wept.

I wish I could say the events of trauma ended here, but three days later, Romeo had nothing planned toward

Esther's funeral. My son-in-law, Paul, adored Esther, but after months of mounting anger he'd reached his tipping point. He invited a close friend, and took action.

Like raging bulls, they headed to Romeo's house with the intention of executing bodily harm. Evidence of Paul's fury spilled out as he charged onto the gravel driveway spraying pebbles on the side lawn. He brought his truck to an abrupt halt as he wrenched open his door.

But as his foot hit the ground a supernatural calm engulfed him. An aura of tranquility became a palpable entity similar to the light Esther's presence brought into a room. Like mist when the sun rises, his anger dissipated.

In a storage building behind their rental home the door to Romeo's office stood open. Calm and purposeful, Paul entered. "Why haven't you started setting up Esther's Memorial Service?" he demanded. Not waiting for an answer, Paul snatched up the phone and thrust it into Romeo's hand. "Call Pastor John *now* and reserve the church for her funeral." Romeo made the call.

His narrative of the event left me in awe again of God's mercy. Physical violence would have only brought a temporary venting, but with it, more trauma for us all.

Considering all of his threats to expose *our* evil, we had no idea what Romeo might plan to do during the service. He did love an audience, so Seth, Melissa (our counselor), and I met with Pastor John and gave him some background. If trouble erupted, at least he would be prepared to shut it down.

Jack gave the sermon instead of Pastor John; our one request regarding the funeral deliberately ignored.

The knots in my stomach twisted and tightened daily as the possible horrifying scenarios gyrated through my mind. *Maybe we shouldn't even go to the funeral. Perhaps we should walk out when Jack starts to speak.* As we discussed different ways to display our disapproval, anything we did to protest would dishonor Esther.

In an effort to bring sanity to the situation, we contacted Jack and asked to meet with him and Candy to smooth out misunderstandings and request him to step down from speaking at the funeral. Candy was willing to meet, but Jack refused.

Romeo called and said he needed Esther's childhood pictures and another person to give a eulogy. Prompted earlier in the week with an idea for a personal tribute, I seized the chance and said, "I'd like to give one titled 'Esther's Beginnings'."

I desired to give people who'd heard Romeo's rumors, especially those who didn't know us, a chance to experience who Seth and I were. I made copies of two special pictures and sent them to the media team at the church. The photos were of five-year-old Esther kneeling with her Daddy after she'd invited Jesus into her heart. At the appropriate time in my eulogy, I would signal them to be shown.

☺☺☺

The day of the funeral I entered the church foyer, fragile as a delicate piece of fine crystal, vulnerable and at risk of shattering by a simple careless tap. With nerves raw and jittery, just standing took great effort. As I glanced up, *life-sized* pictures of Esther plastered the walls of the lobby. The shock caused my knees to buckle. Candy, of all people, stood nearby and caught me by the elbow to stabilize me. I groaned and immediately looked down shielding my eyes. With my hand held in a low salute to block the view of any more pictures I made my way to the pastor's office. Repulsed at the garish display, I thought, *Esther would have hated to appear like a goddess in a shrine to be worshipped.*

I looked at the program and found I was speaker number five, even though my subject was Esther's *beginnings*. I told pastor John, "I'll never make it through this if I can't speak first." He rearranged it and said, "No problem, people often make last minute changes."

I had people praying for me to have a *calm heart*, a *clear mind* and a *strong voice*. To get through this would be a miracle. Who speaks at their own child's funeral?

Marmie's Eulogy

By faith, I got up out of my seat and walked to the platform. A row of prayer warriors lined the pew behind me. A sense of peace covered me, but I faltered as I looked out at the audience. A packed auditorium met my gaze. People occupied every square foot of space. Later, I heard some people couldn't get in the doors.

I shared the story of God's timing regarding Esther's birth. At a right to life conference, God gave me a strong knowing in my spirit I should have another baby. Between extreme morning sickness with my first two daughters and my second-born with special needs, it wasn't something I wanted to hear. But the knowing in my spirit became a certainty. I made a plan to be pregnant by June of 1981 and fortified my body with nutrients to ward off debilitating nausea this time. Well, Esther was born in June of 1981. I've heard it said, "God gets quite a chuckle from our plan-making."

Seth had just lost his mother the first of October and his grief hung like unwanted cobwebs. In late October at my annual gynecology check-up, I received the shocking news, "You're pregnant!" So much for *my* plans. When I shared the news with Seth, his grief lifted like a curtain of dark clouds after a storm. From the beginning Esther's life brought light and joy.

I finished and realized all three of my prayers were answered, from a clear mind to a calm heart and strong voice. I choked up only once, but managed to continue.

As each eulogy was given it became evident Esther's life was so beautiful and walked out with such extraordinary love and grace toward all...no one could mar this service.

Toward the end of Romeo's eulogy, a recording of Esther singing floated across the auditorium—melodies and lyrics of two songs she'd written. My heart staggered at the unexpected sound of her sweet unpretentious voice. Instead of the comfort it should have brought, it *felt* like a cruel plot to intensify the pain of my loss.

As Jack started his sermon, I could not look at him. Jayne and I both bowed our heads and as inconspicuous as possible, put our fingers in our ears. I could not acknowledge this display of arrogance and disrespect to our sweet Esther.

The two separate greeting lines at the end of the service were the only evidence of the great chasm between our family and Romeo. Our wounds fresh, no words passed between us.

As I walked out of the auditorium, I realized amidst all the flowers and orchids, I hadn't seen her urn of ashes, so I returned to the front of the church. I needed one last caress, even if separated by a ceramic container. Aghast, the absence of its existence inserted another blade of sorrow. Such a dishonor to her memory, I could only shake my head. After an area search of funeral homes, we discovered Romeo had not even picked up her ashes. They remained on a shelf in a box. Although we'd been blocked from picking them up, we called daily. Weeks later they were gone, so we assumed Romeo had them. To this day we have no urn, gravesite, or place to mourn.

Cassidy, Esther's niece, who volunteered to be Esther's surrogate for her child, texted Romeo on two different occasions and requested a few of her ashes to swirl in a special crafted necklace she wanted as a keepsake. He never responded.

Two weeks later, a much-needed Memorial Service of celebration was held. Our family gathered from across the country plus many local friends. Each one a gift and heartwarming hug to our souls. With hands raised our songs of praise lightened our brokenness as worship music filled the air. A piano/vocal solo "Going Home" was performed by a personal music colleague and friend.

He composed the piece for a friend who'd lost their child. The service honored our dear girl and helped begin a long road of healing. Her sister Jayne, cousin Nevin, a friend from the Ukraine, a student from Dark 2 Light, and I, gave the eulogies. Our Pastor brought beautiful healing words in his shepherd-hearted compassionate way.

With family and friends surrounding us, Esther's closing chapter found her sixth grade teacher, once again lending her buoyant spirit to us as she used Sign Language to close out Esther's Memorial Service with the dramatic worship song *Glorious Day*, by Casting Crowns.

Esther's prayers and heart's desire for her family to become God's masterpiece continue, only in another dimension.

REFLECT

Have you ever experienced a loved one whose suffering became so intense and extended you pleaded for the Lord to take them home?

APPLY

I've prayed for release by physical death for two of the most precious people in my life. My Mother who endured Alzheimer's for almost twenty years, then again with Esther when her suffering became so great. This is why...

Jesus repeated the words, *fear not*, to His disciples many times through stories and miracles, but they didn't get it until He was resurrected from the dead. Then his followers became *fearless* and changed the world.
Because I didn't fear their death, I could ask God to take them home.

> *It's very difficult to threaten people*
> *who are not afraid of death.*
> Andy Stanley

On YouTube, listen to Andy's series "You're Not the Boss of Me" Part 5.

PRAYER

Father, thank you for the confidence I have in you through your Son, Jesus, who not only lived out a perfect life of truth in love, but suffered the worst imaginable death. Then when all looked hopeless, He conquered death which gives me the opportunity to walk in unshakeable fearlessness; even to losing my own life *or* that of a loved one.

Chapter 49

Forgiveness...A Journey to Freedom

The *heart* of this book is the ability to forgive—not just by choice from the head, but from a transformation of the heart. If you rush through the next stories you may miss the joy and freedom available to every follower of Jesus Christ.

Grief and tragedies come with questions, guilt, regrets and blame. *What if I'd?* ... *How could you?... If only*.... you fill in the blank.

The following six stories are the landmark events which shaped my journey to heart forgiveness and peace.

May they help guide you on yours.

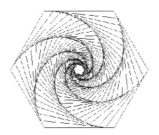

Part 1
Drowning in Sorrow and Anger

With some vengeance as fuel, I scraped together enough energy to survive my first days of grief. I longed for validation for Seth and me. We *were* loving parents. I longed to set the record straight and reveal how our family had been cruelly wronged and slandered.

To escape the relentless negative energy which stalked me, I hiked a nearby trail. Droplets of grief streaked my cheeks and fell to the ground as I cut my way through a wooded path bordering a Civil War battlefield. Wind through pine boughs mimicked cries of fallen soldiers—a fitting backdrop to my war-torn heart. My first autumn without Esther to share the colorful wonder of the season shrouded my heart in dull gray. Would my trail of tears never end?

I continued to tromp through fields as I felt the strong prod once again, *you must record Esther's story.* I thought, *how can I tell her story besieged by so much hurt and anger?* My deepest desire in writing it required I reveal God's amazing glory and abiding grace; yet honesty made it necessary to expose my valid fury without it smudging the narrative. My goal—to redeem the ashes of sorrow and pain while revealing God,

Emmanuel, who walked *with* and comforted me over the long arduous journey.

As I *chose* forgiveness by my will, a snail-paced progression of healing began, but at this point bitterness still tinged my heart with vengeful ugly thoughts. Evidence revealed itself every time I thought or spoke of Esther's Romeo. My toxic words, even if deserved, flowed with spite and very little mercy.

My hike and release of tears drained some of the hostility and left me humbled. In the quiet of my bedroom with body prostrate, and forehead pressed hard, an imprint of rug pattern left evidence of the intense inner battle. Fuzz-tickled nose, tear-stained cheeks and sodden tissues surrounded me as the murderous hatred surged once again. The intensity frightened me as internal alarms clanked an inner warning—*forgive or **you'll** be destroyed.*

As I walked out this zig-zag, see-saw existence, I found restorative mercy to be a process—a circuitous multi-layered journey where the depth of pain dictated the length of time required.

Forgiveness, a familiar word, floated beyond my grasp; a vague concept on a distant horizon.

Part 2

The Hiding Place

Betsie implored Corrie, "Tell people what we

have learned here. There is no pit so deep

that He is not deeper still!"

I *also* desired the ashes of Esther's suffering to demonstrate *there is no pit so deep that He is not deeper still.*

When I shared my massive ongoing struggle to forgive those who hurt Esther and our family so unjustly with a wise friend, she suggested: "Marla, go back and re-read *The Hiding Place.* I think it might communicate the words you need to hear as you walk out your own vast injustice and pain."

If you're familiar with the book and film, "The Hiding Place," by Corrie ten Boom, you'll recognize those names and remember the resulting breadth of their worldwide ministry. The pit Betsie spoke of was Ravensbruck, a Nazi concentration camp during WW II, where they experienced horrors of indescribable suffering. Corrie's release came as a result of a clerical error resulting in freedom rather than execution. Her sister, Betsie, died there.

The tender compassionate heart of Betsie penetrated and convicted my own. She had what I'd call a heavenly-heart with Jesus-vision. The type Jesus revealed when he spoke from the cross.

Father, forgive them, for they know not what they do.

Betsie not only ministered to the broken victims, but she ached for the dreadful bankrupt souls and suffering of her jailers—those who were so harsh to the innocents. Betsie saw the big picture of God's kingdom from the book of Matthew:

Thy kingdom come;

Thy will be done. In earth as it is in heaven.

Corrie ten Boom wrote a letter to the Dutchman who betrayed her family to the Nazi's, revealing how his actions had caused the death of her beloved father and sister without hiding the truth or her anger.

She also told him, "the harm you planned for us, surprisingly, served to push me *closer* to God."

I thought, *Corrie, how did you do it? How could anyone come through that much relentless, long-term horror and even death— stay sane, survive, and then forgive?!*

My struggle to forgive Romeo from the heart skittered and slithered away from me time after time. Rays of mercy and forgiveness disappeared as dark clouds of grief, anger, and revenge rolled in and blotted out the light. Even though I'd *chosen* multiple times by *my will* to forgive, the tentacles of pain and loss tripped me up and sucked me back in.

Part 3

Miracles from Heaven

Sometime after Esther's homegoing, I'd just seen the movie, *Miracles from Heaven*—a true story about Anna, a young girl who had a rare incurable digestive disorder. While playing in an old tree in her front yard, a limb snapped and she'd fallen thirty feet head first into a dead hollowed-out cottonwood and rendered unconscious. Frantic attempts to rescue her failed.

In desperation, friends and family circled the tree and laid their hands on the huge trunk as they recited the Lord's Prayer aloud. Eventually rescued and rushed to the hospital, an examination by the medical team found she'd only suffered a mild concussion—a true miracle. Later, Anna said she had an encounter with God. Her incurable digestive disease also disappeared. Yet the scene of people surrounding the tree and praying the Lord's Prayer aloud gripped me over anything else in her miraculous story.

A few days later, I sat in a women's leadership meeting. My friend, Tammy, opened the meeting. Her prayer glowed with a unique power as she intricately threaded segments of The Lord's Prayer throughout it. Later she shared how revolutionary a new book titled, *21 Seconds to Change Your World,* had been to her. The book's theme centered around the Lord's Prayer. It takes approximately *21 seconds* to recite it. I went home and ordered the book.

The author, Mark Rutland, a pastor, speaker, and New York Times bestselling author, had fallen into a slimy pit of black depression. In that low place, a lie out of the darkness seemed to whisper—*You don't have a prayer!* Just as quick, another thought challenged, *Yes, you do! You have a prayer if you will learn to use it.* Mark embraced The Lord's Prayer until...

...it came alive in me. I breathed it. I marinate my poor brain in it.

I said it multiple times a day, ...I clung to it,

...as a drowning man clings to a raft in the middle of a storm...

It was my meat, my friend, my comfort in the night.

I meditated on it, ...cherished its words, its structure,

its brilliant and magnificently anointed economy of language.

Not a syllable is wasted, ... Its power is supernatural.

As I walked out the summer deeply missing Esther's presence, The Lord's Prayer graced my lips when I woke, and as I fell asleep. I repeated it over and over as I swam laps, as I prepared meals, on my walks, when I made the bed or took a shower.

Gradually my heart became lighter and more peaceful. I searched my soul for the raging vengeance which had tenaciously clung. A sense of wholeness and calm birthed hope of one day experiencing the reality of a *heart* forgiveness.

For the word of God is alive and active.

Sharper than any double-edged sword... Hebrews 4:12

Part 4

Soul Memories

Several years have elapsed since Esther's home going and I recollect my walk at the battlefield. I re-examine those tear droplets which felt like streams of oozing acid, and I've found some have transformed into precious jewels of compassion and wisdom.

I discovered time is a necessary ingredient to heal malice and soul scars. Until one is far enough down the road of mourning, there's not enough distance to look back and see the big picture clearly. As with the visual defect of myopia, our sight of the event is clouded. Pain and sorrow blind us when it's too fresh and close up.

Hours of reviewing Esther's journals, e-mails, and pictures, as I wrote her story, would often leave me emotionally drained. The days of summer were hardest because her last one was full of suffering and many traumatic events—but July was the most difficult.

During a July after her death I purposefully started a Journal of Joy. A place to record moments of hope, thankfulness, smiles, and God-moments from my day—no matter how small.

Calmly swimming laps at the pool, bubbles of grief exploded as I unexpectedly started a keening wail just before lifting my face from the water. From a place deep within, a tidal wave of sadness erupted. Thankful I was alone, the sobs eventually subsided, as I asked myself, *what just happened?* I'd had no conscious thoughts of Esther or sadness, but later as I pondered the powerful incident, I concluded it had to be a *soul memory* surfacing.

I checked my journal and found Esther had entered the hospital for the last time on this day four years before. Such an *unholy day*, as we'd been cut off from all medical updates.

It began the most heartbreaking ten days of our family's lives. During this time, a saturated agony ripped through my soul until I thought my heart would physically explode. Yet strangely, a profound time of experiencing God's presence coincided with the anguish. His tender mercies and miracles of grace layered over me like a liquid balm.

I *experienced* Psalm 34:18:

The LORD is close to the brokenhearted and saves those who are crushed in spirit.

Part 5

Root of Bitterness

On a lovely Sunday morning in September 2017, a peaceful presence encircled me as I lingered on our deck at first light waiting for the sun to rise. I sang the worship song "Holy Spirit You Are Welcome Here" as wispy breezes tossed my hair and caressed my face.

My cell phone chimed. I glanced down. A new morning inspiration from Faith Gateway had come in featuring a portion of a new book, "The Christian Atheist" by Craig Groeschel. The title grabbed my attention, but the subtitle, "When You Believe in God, But Won't Forgive," caused me to say— "Ouch!"

My mood shifted as I glared at the sky. Frustrated, I muttered through gritted teeth, "Lord, I'm so tired of struggling with forgiveness!"

But I had just welcomed the Holy Spirit into my space and knew this was no coincidence. The verse in large print at the beginning of the article glared at me: *Forgive, just as Christ forgave you.* Ephesians 4:32

I'd labored and groveled for years as I'd inched my way toward a core forgiveness for Esther's Romeo. I'd chosen repeatedly by my *will* to forgive, but my *heart* was still captive to the sorrow and hurt of his vicious lies and betrayal. My blame and anger were honest and my desire for justice, right and understandable. Wrong forgiven is still wrong done, yet a thorn of ire still festered in my spirit.

Craig, the author, shared his story. His parents presented him the birthday gift of his younger sister, born on his third birthday, as a gift from God. This cherished sister became his best friend as they shared life together. Unknown to him until he was an adult, his beloved sister had been molested repeatedly by a close family friend who was both teacher and coach. His words hit close to home and were raw and honest:

"To say that I wanted Max to die and burn in hell doesn't even begin to convey how much I wanted him to suffer. Although the words rage, hate, and revenge come to mind when I think about Max, the English language simply doesn't have a word for what I felt."

I so identified with his statement, and like Craig, I reasoned our family's suffering had to be an exception until I read the following verse from Hebrews:

See to it that no one falls short of the grace of God

And that no bitter root grows up to cause trouble and defile many.

Hebrews 12:15 NIV

The eyes of my soul opened with the realization, *my* struggle with forgiveness lay in a root of bitterness also. Yet, it *felt* so right. It's frightening how easy it is to justify such acidic poison. The tell-tale signs were my thoughts and words which played the painful events over and over —keeping detailed accounts.

A lightning bolt of memory struck. Romeo's first words from his eulogy echoed and grated. I Corinthians 13 is considered the "Love Chapter" of the Bible. To hear those words coming from his mouth at the funeral, the one who had treated us and our daughter with such selfishness, contention and abuse felt blasphemous. I wanted to rise from my seat, rip his tongue out, scratch out his eyes, and scream! I bowed my head low and shut him out, but one phrase from verse five caught me with a twinge of conviction, *Love keeps no record of wrongs.*

Regardless of the justification for my bitterness, God's word left no room for it. He loved and desired good things for me and this bitterness thwarted his good plans for my life.

Craig's story continued: "When we found out that Max had been diagnosed with muscular dystrophy, I naturally concluded God was giving him his due. But when anyone celebrates another person's diagnoses of a crippling disease, it's time for a heart check."

Week after week God brought conviction to Craig through timely sermons and personal Bible study. I'd experienced similar promptings.

Ephesians 4:31-32 states the only way to eliminate the root is through forgiveness. *Get rid of all bitterness, rage and anger, brawling and slander, along with every form of malice. Be kind and compassionate to one another, forgiving each other, just as in Christ God forgave you.*

In Luke 6:28, Jesus teaches us to—*bless those who curse you, pray for those who mistreat you.*

Matthew 5:43-44, *You have heard that it was said, 'Love your neighbor and hate your enemy.' But I tell you: Love your enemies and pray for those who persecute you.*

My heart recoiled...how does one wrap their mind around such a concept?

As Craig's story unfolded, he began with great angst to pray a short unemotional prayer for Max. "God, I pray you work in his life." Over time Craig's heart softened. The battle to forgive bounced back and forth between revenge and forgiveness. Eventually Craig wrote Max a letter forgiving him and outlining the plan of salvation. This resulted in Max's salvation five days before he died. The power of forgiveness is radical.

The sun rose full as I finished reading Craig's penetrating article. An intense Holy Spirit conviction summoned my heart—it was time to deal with *my* root of bitterness.

The greatest challenge I've wrestled with is, "how do I *truly* forgive?" My heart and soul were so battle weary. As I've stated, forgiveness is a process. But it seemed I was on a treadmill, covering the same territory:

Anger!

    Revenge!

        Conviction.

            Surrender.

                Repentance.

                    Relief.

                        Anger!

Further comments by Craig Groeschel gave me some needed clarity: *Forgiving others often starts as a decision of surrender—an act of our will. This surrender invites God to* ***begin*** *working in our lives at a deeper level, allowing God to heal us.* (emphasis mine.)

I'd chosen to forgive Romeo over and over, yet I didn't have heart peace or soul freedom.

As Craig succinctly stated, my surrender of *choosing* to forgive invited God to work in my life at a deeper level. It wasn't a treadmill, but a long rocky climb up a mountain of sorrow.

I'd been pulling out the acidic leaves of vengeance by my will, *choosing* to forgive—but to kill a tenacious plant, you have to remove the root, or it returns. I finished Craig's story with somber conviction, and knew it was time to delve into the cesspool in my own heart.

Part 6

Letter to Romeo

Monday morning dawned bright and clear as I began writing a letter to Romeo. Immediately I came to an impasse. This forgiveness business was hard if not impossible. I prayed for direction and then decided to go back and review the video of Esther's Memorial Service. I hadn't listened to Romeo's eulogy at the time or even looked at him. Now, I knew I needed to hear his words, see his body language, his facial expressions and experience it fully to completely forgive.

Much time had passed since I'd experienced this service in person. I braced myself as I stared at the computer screen and with an unsteady hand clicked the start button.

My eyes traced his familiar figure. Dressed in shades of black from raven hair to his ebony shoes; new growth of a dark beard etched his face. A countenance of wearied sadness oozed a hopeless desolation of soul and I couldn't help but hurt for him. He had a skewed view of their marriage but his words recognized the beauty and light of their life together came from Esther and her faith. All spiritual elements focused on her. There were no personal words of faith in Christ or hope of heaven.

A window of light opened in my soul—a new capacity of love, along with a deep sadness for him. I struggled to write a few more lines in his letter but again bogged down in the drivel I found coming from my pen.

☉☉☉

I reviewed Corrie ten Boom's story of forgiving the Nazi guard who was so cruel to she and her sister while imprisoned in the concentration camp of Ravensbruck. In 1947 after the war, Corrie was speaking at a church in Munich, Germany, sharing her story with the message that God forgives. "He casts our sin into the deepest ocean, gone forever."

After the service, her worst nightmare stood before her! The Nazi guard from Ravensbruck. "You mentioned Ravensbruck in your talk," he was saying. "I was a guard there, but since then, I've become a Christian. I know God has forgiven me for the cruel things I did, but I'd like to hear it from your lips as well, Fraulein." The horrors of his cruelty scrolled through her mind as he thrust his arm forward to shake her hand asking, "will you forgive me?"

"I stood there—I whose sins had to be forgiven every day—and could not. Betsie had died in that place—could he erase her slow terrible death simply for the asking?"

(I so identified with Corrie, as I'd watched my beloved Esther have pain meds withheld and treated so callously by Romeo and those he'd convinced of our supposed evil.)

The seconds ticked by, but felt like hours as Corrie wrestled with the most difficult decision of her life. She'd worked with many victims of Nazi cruelty and only those who could forgive former enemies rebuilt meaningful lives. If they nursed their bitterness, they remained invalids.

With an icy heart, anger clutched tight but she knew the *choice* of forgiveness did not require emotion. "Jesus, help me!" she prayed silently. "I can lift my hand. I can do that much. You supply the feeling."

The stilted movement of her hand met the guards and God provided the fireworks of emotion as a current of joy and celebration exploded down her arm and into her heart. A healing warmth coupled with tears accompanied her words, "I forgive you brother, with all my heart!" Corrie stated, "I'd never known God's love as intensely as I did at that moment."

ⓔⓔⓔ

Not having an address for Romeo, I didn't know if my letter would ever reach him, but I knew *I* needed healing regardless. I only wrote one page on Monday as the internal struggle of forgiveness twisted and roiled. Tuesday, I wrote another half-page. This wasn't going well. "Hard! Hard! Hard!" I wrote in my journal. "Lord, help!"

My impetus to keep pressing toward the goal of heart forgiveness was this—when internal thoughts of returning evil for evil reigned, I found evil overcame *me*.

Forgiveness and cleansing from anger and hatred comes at a high price.

I had to give up the right to get even.

Jerry Sitzer

Do not be overcome by evil, but overcome evil with good.

Romans 12:2

Wednesday, at 4:30 a.m., I woke to the words, "You're not being honest!"

I asked, "What? What do you mean, Lord?"

I knew it was God's Spirit as He often spoke to me during the twilight moments of waking. "You're not being honest about Romeo's offenses against you. Your gift of mercy is getting in the way. When I called Israel out on their sin, I didn't mince words. I named it loud and clear through my prophets."

I eased myself out of bed and went to my Bible lying in my favorite kitchen nook. I randomly opened it and Isaiah chapter nine, with the sub-title, "The Lord's Anger

Against Israel," stared back at me. Startled, my heart faltered.

God's prophet *didn't* mince words or ignore the sins of the people. He laid out their sin and consequences in vivid detail. I realized my letter had been too milquetoast and timid; I needed to roar out all the pain. How can I truly forgive what I won't acknowledge? How can I forgive if I don't face the depth of gross evil done to me?

By 4:45 a.m. the cruelty perpetrated against myself, Esther and our family, splattered over the page. By the end of the day I had finished. Five single-spaced pages laid before me. As I wrote…my own sins were revealed and purged as well. "Hmm," I questioned after a few paragraphs, "Am I writing this as much for my own cleansing?" Tears of repentance fell periodically throughout the day.

My prayer at the end of the letter read, "Lord, I don't want to drag this unforgiveness corpse around anymore. Help me to see Romeo through your eyes. Please do a complete work of forgiveness in my heart for Romeo. I lay it at the foot of your cross." Then I saw why I couldn't shake off the toxic weight of bitterness. It wasn't *humanly* possible. Let me say that again louder, "It wasn't *humanly* possible!"

"Lord," I said, "by my will I *choose* to forgive, but Holy Spirit, you'll have to do the heart surgery for me *emotionally*. Please take this bitterness from me."

I can't explain it, but I felt the weight gradually lift, and sensed it veer toward the ceiling and dissipate. My heart, a helium balloon of joy and airy lightness drifted into an atmosphere of love. The first words out of my mouth were a sincere, "Lord, how do you want me to pray for Romeo?" A miracle had occurred; these words did not come from a bitter spiteful heart.

Instantly the words came, "Thy kingdom come, thy will be done *in Romeo* as it is in heaven." My hands raised in victory. I knew this thought, this prayer hadn't come from me. I realized I was in the midst of another miracle. The prayer, so succinct and powerful.

The words of the Lord's Prayer are interpreted either: "thy will be done **in** (or **on**) earth as it is in heaven,"

*Then the Lord God formed a man from the **dust of the ground** and breathed*

into his nostrils the breath of life, and the man became a living being. (emphasis mine)

Genesis 2:7 NIV

We *are* formed from the dust of the earth. Thy will be done *in* Romeo made sense.

I immediately prayed the simple phrase over Romeo. Penetrating words flooded my mind from James 5:16, *the prayer of a righteous person is powerful and effective.* My spirit felt something shift in the heavenly realms. A confirmation to me the Lord heard and would act.

Romeo was still responsible for his own choices, but I knew I was free!

Experiencing soul freedom is a rare jewel—a peace-filled heart of lightness and joy.

I felt Esther's smile.

Forgiving people let God rule the universe.

Jerry Sitzer

Chapter 50

From Heaven's Point of View

My Dear Marmie,

I know your suffering has been beyond description during the last months of my life and especially now during our physical separation. Even though I'm with Jesus, I feel the loss of you too. The big picture is now clear to me, so I'm not sad or grieving as you are, but I see your struggle and heartache. I'm cheering you on with our loved ones and many others in the great cloud of witnesses Hebrews 12 speaks of.

During my last few weeks on earth I grieved for all who loved me so well, but were kept from me. Divided, slandered by deceived, well-intentioned friends and, sadly, led by my husband. God knows your suffering and the lack of closure with me before I made this journey to my heavenly home.

Marmie, you and I were so close, like two bodies sharing the same soul, sensitive to the art and beauty of the world around us and tuned in to God's heart. We simply *got* each other. We both loved the outdoors because what we found there became springboards to worship the God who created it.

When I heard Aunt Katrina offer you the condo at Myrtle Beach, a place where I felt so at home, I went straight to Jesus and asked if we could plan a special day for you.

Your trip to Myrtle Beach would eventually seal the truth of how God's deliberate presence and comfort would be part of every story in your book, because grief is *not* our future.

The sun-kissed glow on your faces as you, Aunt Katrina, and my dear sister Jayne waited for a table at the restaurant, let me know you had begun to relax and renew. The sun, vast ocean breezes, and freedom from months of battle gave you energy to smile and laugh again. Nearby, I watched you snap pictures in the pre-sunset light. Your tanned relaxed faces were wreathed in smiles. Later, the special photos spoke loud of your peace and the inner healing taking place.

You shared a giant margarita at dinner and devoured delicious seafood. How we loved sharing times of yummy food and conversation, Marmie. I miss that and look forward to a time when we'll do it once again in grand style—at the Marriage Supper of the Lamb, the ultimate meal.

Back at the condo, you played the dice game Farkle. You tried to decide if the word was obscene or just fun to say. Your belly-laughs ignited my own joy. A euphoric happiness permeated your evening.

ⓔⓔⓔ

The next morning, I couldn't wait for you to get to the beach. Jesus and I had such splendid plans laid out for you.

While you set up your beach towels, chairs and umbrella, Jesus and I went to work. Aunt Katrina beach-combed while you and Jayne grabbed your boogie boards and headed into the water. I smiled as you frolicked, catching wave after wave. Jesus had beckoned a giant school of feeder fish to the area, and from far out at sea He summoned a group of much larger specimens.

To complete our plan, we needed to get you out of the water. Did you notice the unusual pattern as rain approached from both north and south? There was a reason for that. We needed to make sure you were safe on shore. You noticed the approaching storms first and alerted Jayne. Grabbing your towels, you ran and found cover just as the downpour started.

Only short-lived squalls…you were soon back on the beach. I observed your trio, like turtles on a log, stretch out on mats and waggle your bodies into comfortable positions. The fun was about to begin. I clapped for joy as my anticipation mounted.

I watched your eyes scan the ocean as the fish started jumping. You stood up. You knew from years of vacations at the ocean, when small fish were leaping, large ones were feasting. You expressed surprise at the unusual feeding time of noon, rather than their normal early morning or evening schedule. That wasn't coincidence either.

I watched Jesus raise his hand, much like the trainers do when signaling a dolphin to leap in the air. Like a bomb, fish catapulted in every direction, followed by a large shark hurtling five feet into the air. Whoa! Marmie, I wish you could have seen your expression! A look of fascination mixed with terror passed over your face and you exclaimed, "That's right where we were swimming!" I applauded, but you stood mesmerized. Sharks continued to vault high out of the ocean and attack in a frenzied display of raw nature for the next thirty minutes.

Later, I tagged along as you headed to the mall for some retail therapy. Like little girls playing dress up, you loaded your carts with possibilities and spent two hours trying on outfits. With good humor you made fun of each other, or *Ooo'd* and *Ahh'd* over your special finds.

Back at the condo I lay beside you when you stretched out to ease your aching back. Too much boogie boarding maybe? The fun was just beginning, so I left to check in with Jesus and see how our next project was coming together.

I returned as Jesus directed the head dolphin of the largest local pod to pay *you* a special visit. I can travel at the speed of thought now, so literally in a flash I returned to your condo to watch it play out. Katrina and Jayne prepared taco salad in the kitchen. You dragged the coffee table to the balcony and set it for supper. You glanced over the rail and spied the lone head dolphin as he came straight toward shore. He seemed to know when you noticed him as he quickly turned and headed back out to sea. After all, he had work to do. You remarked, "Oh my! Sharks *and* a friendly dolphin. How special!"

Tummies grumbled their hunger, but as you sat down to eat, a muffled *boom* sounded. The sky darkened and the rumbling turned into full-on thunder and lightning. The beach quickly emptied but the high tide was about to wash your belongings out to sea. You scrambled down fourteen floors and ran across the beach as rain pelted, lightening flashed, and thunder roared. You gathered your sand-encrusted beach gear to a safe area to retrieve later.

Flushed cheeks and shortness of breath were the only evidence of your adventure as you returned to your taco salad. (Sorry about the necessary scary storm to get your attention, but Jesus and I had you covered.)

Just as you settled back on the balcony, bright sunlight flashed behind you. The storm still passed in front of the balcony, but immediately you jumped up and exclaimed, "Rainbow! There's going to be a rainbow!" Special symbols to me of God's promises, I knew you'd get the significance, and you did. The rainbow formed and it's center like a healing balm rose from the ocean right in front of you. You can be sure the placement was specific and purposeful.

Katrina and Jayne returned their empty plates to the kitchen as you sat down to finish eating. Jesus lingered to your right and like a conductor raised both arms as if ready to begin a symphony. I sat on the balcony railing grinning like a Cheshire cat as you caught the first movement of dark objects off to your right. You mused aloud, "Oh, I guess the sharks are back." You continued to watch as the form of a dolphin leaped clear of the water. You snatched up your binoculars and brought them into focus as four dolphins jumped into the air in perfect unison.

Your cries of pleasure brought Aunt Katrina and Jayne running. Jaws dropped and your childlike glee rode the air waves. My joy at your delight spilled out in my own sparkling, heavenly laughter. I wish you could have heard it. Yet I knew by your face you felt it. Dolphins by the dozens filled the sea before us, a show better than anything Disney had to offer. You walked back into the condo with eyes wide. You seemed overcome with awe as you slapped your hands against your cheeks and exclaimed, 'Oh my, ladies, God sure outdid Himself today! Do you think Esther and Jesus planned this for us?'

Yes, Marmie! You got it! I danced. I twirled. I jumped up and down and applauded.

Jayne and Katrina called their husbands, but you returned to the balcony to watch the last remnant of the rainbow. Although earthbound, you knew a celestial scene when you saw one as the end of the rainbow disintegrated into a shimmering cascade of watery light and flowed into the sea. You tried to get Jayne and Katrina's attention but they were absorbed in their phone conversations.

Since this next event had been planned specifically for you, I watched as you stood mesmerized; enraptured by the beauty of the one lone cloud as it formed at the base of the fading waterfall. It mushroomed and a bright coral light arose from its center like a beautiful flower. Quick as a fiddler crab, you scurried inside and grabbed your cell phone. I knew what was next, but I had to leave you for a moment to finish my role in this day.

From a distance I observed your return to the balcony. The cloud's coral color had faded, but you snapped a picture anyway. When you stepped back into the condo, I'd returned just as you brought the picture up to view. I thought you would fall as you stumbled and through a gasping whisper exclaimed, 'Esther's face is in the middle of the cloud!'

Aunt Katrina studied it and simply responded, 'Well, I don't see it.' When you showed the photo to Jayne she said, 'Umm…I see something that looks like Ronald McDonald.' Annoyed, you retorted, 'How can you not see her, it's *all* I can see!' Again, I giggled with delight!

Marmie, I wanted there to be no doubt, Jesus and I planned this moment just for *you*. I know you cry many tears for me, but share my joy, for I am free. Hear my voice in a song. Feel my touch on a breeze. Listen for my laughter to cheer you. Be aware, for I am near. Now it's time to let me go and share our story of God's faithfulness with the world."

Esther

The tranquility of soul which I experienced at Myrtle Beach encased and swirled around me like an airy gossamer veil as I traveled home. But when I walked through the door of my house, vibrations of unexpected grief slowly gathered momentum, and like a landslide of rocks tumbling down a mountainside—buried me. Falling into my Seth's arms I sobbed loud,

"Oh, no! I feel like I just lost Esther *again!*"

At the beach I'd thought, *this grief experience won't be so bad. After all, I've worked through most of the painful events as I experienced them.* Yes, unrealistic— but during the moment, still under the enchantment of ocean, glorious sunrises and sunsets, and cloaked in the supernatural peace of God-moments, it seemed possible.

I didn't realize the *time* healing would take as I had a long valley of heartache to walk out. Still, the events at the beach would sustain me and be a constant encouragement.

Over the next weeks my daughter, Jayne, called frequently, often with an invitation:

"Hey Mom, why don't you and Dad come over for supper tonight? Paul is grilling steaks."

Paul, Jayne's husband, is a *master* of the grill. I'd even bought him a hat for his July birthday with the words, "Grills Love Me," embroidered on the front.

In our after-dinner conversation I asked Paul to look at the picture of the cloud where I saw Esther's face. I wanted someone else to experience what I had. His explosive gasp as I brought up the picture on my phone, caused my heart to leap.

"Do *you* see her?" I gushed.

"You mean the large eye in the top right-hand corner?"

Puzzled, I responded, "Huh? What eye?"

Then, like a blindfold falling away, it emerged. How had I missed it? Although Paul hadn't seen Esther's face, an epiphany unveiled itself as lyrics of an old hymn scrolled across my mind. "His eye is on the sparrow, and I know He watches me."

My laughter erupted as I exclaimed: "Yes! Esther and Jesus *were* together!"

I felt my smile widen; I think the corners extended to each ear.

Then, another *eureka* moment exploded.

If man can store his pictures in a cloud, how simple for the God who *created* the clouds.

Later as I reminisced on our beach week, I remembered watching the full moon rise on our last night. The rays of light extending from the moon created a perfect cross. This beautiful Jesus-Esther-hug, sealed a week of sweet memories to keep close as I walked out my future days of grief in hope.

The heavens declare the glory of God; the skies proclaim the work of his hands.

Psalm 19:1a

If there's one repeated theme throughout Esther's story it's encased in Jesus name, **Emmanuel**.

Matthew 1:23

Behold, a virgin shall be with child, and shall bring forth a son,

*and they shall call his name Emmanuel, which being interpreted is, **God with us.***

No matter how dark your journey, God is present. Sometimes his presence will be obvious—other times he'll whisper from the shadows.

My prayer for you, the reader, is to know Jesus as your personal Emmanuel, alive and active, not just in Esther's story but in your own.

A Personal Invitation

Whatever your grief: a loved one's death, a friend's suicide, the loss of your marriage, your employment, or your shattered dreams over a child addicted to drugs—my heart aches for you. Even as you have read this book, know I've prayed over you. Thank you for walking with me through my journey of shattering loss to forgiveness and peace. May you also experience the transforming *truth*...Secure in Christ's finished work on the cross, grief doesn't have to be *your* future either. Even if it feels crazy and untrue, say it with me **LOUD** and **STRONG.**

Grief Is Not My Future!

~ EPILOGUE ~

A universal question is, *why does God allow suffering in the world?*

I'm referring to *all* of it: the horrors of world wars, torture, innocent children starving, killing babies, sex trafficking, and sexual abuse by those who should be protecting them. Women suffering from abusive husbands or vice versa, mistreatment and cruelty to animals, people dying of cancer, and the list goes on.

Believe it or not the Bible reveals the best answer ever given in John 9:1-3. Jesus heals a man, blind from birth. The disciples assume someone in the man's family sinned and caused this. It is true, sometimes a person sins and reaps the consequences. But Jesus explains this man's blindness is not because of him or his family's sin..."

So, you ask, "What caused it?"

When Adam and Eve allowed sin to enter the world, their sin held the door wide open for death, pain, sorrow *and* blindness to come in right behind them. A *global consequence* of sin resulted.

There are two unwieldy truths a Christian must make peace with: In one hand a Christian holds on to *hope* through their *salvation in Christ*, but in the other hand is a *brutal fact*—the harsh reality of *universal sin* in a broken world. If you deny this reality, your faith in Christ and the Bible will be ground to dust.

How did I live through the horror of losing our beloved daughter in the cruelest circumstances, yet endure and survive with my faith in God's goodness intact? Let me introduce you to the ONE who gave me the victory…

Therefore, since we have a great high priest who has ascended into heaven, Jesus the Son of God, let us hold firmly to the faith we profess. For we do not have a high priest who is unable to empathize with our weaknesses, but we have one who has been tempted in every way, just as we are—yet He did not sin. Let us then approach God's throne of grace with confidence, so that we may receive mercy and find grace to help us in our time of need. Hebrews 4:14-16

He is **W**hy, **G**rief is **N**o **L**onger **M**y **F**uture!

ACKNOWLEDGEMENTS

Beth Davis, sliding a timid toe across the threshold of the almost empty room for my *first* ever writing workshop, I spotted you. Your bright countenance and blonde hair stood out like a beacon. I crossed the room and sat down right beside you. We shared our stories and you invited me to your newly formed writers' group. Then you were gracious enough to become my bed and breakfast place once a month after our Friday night meetings. Now, years later, we've accumulated precious memories too many to count. I wish I could adequately express how much I have valued your encouraging words, hospitality, generosity, in depth critiques, and big picture perspectives. I don't believe this book would have found its way to others who mourn, without your support.

Karli Land, a natural leader, and trailblazer of all things literary—thank you for your vision of gathering a few fringe writers together and building an organization which has mushroomed and blessed myself and others beyond words. (Pun intended) You serve others like Jesus, giving freely of yourself to the point of blessing *and* exhaustion. My only regret is not getting to spend *more* time with you.

Paul Moses, thank you so much for your patient leadership of my critique group for so many faithful years. You taught me so much through your skill with words as you painted pictures in my mind of new locales and worlds not of this earth. Your clean writing, wit, and imagination sprinkled laughter and delight throughout every meeting. A "Word Thief" extraordinaire, (and proud of it). You encouraged me at my first timid reading, when you said, "You have some real writing chops!" I floated on air that evening as I traveled home. From our dueling commas to your restrained and kind critiques you helped me stay the course. I can't wait to read your series of Serbius and see them at the movies someday. Yes, they are that good!

David Brown, as a member of my first critique group of 4 you amazed me with the fact you wrote horror but could spin off a sweet children's story with ease. Thank you for your kind patience with me as I poured my own sorrowful memoir on paper. I now smile as I remember you spent a day dreading how to tell me it was too dark. You were right. So today, thanks to you, I have a file of many happy memories plus the poem you wrote for her, The Girl I Didn't Know.

Cheryll Snow, you presented a workshop on Point of View (POV) to our small band of authors-to-be. So new to the art, I had no idea what you were talking about. If you could have X-rayed my brain activity, the rotating question marks would have made you dizzy. Your handouts of some basic writing guide lines and rules have never been far out of reach ever since.

Experiencing the launch of your first book, Sea Horses, and watching you soar has been a great delight. Our weekend critique soiree's at Beth's gave me some of the best insights into writing as you helped me to rearranged words and make them sparkle. You light up my pages and my life.

Vickie McEntire, what a treasure you are. I've watched, listened, and learned so much from you. You were a highlight of my critique group experiences; not only a wonderful writer but you were quick to see the promotional opportunity beyond the page. You pulled marketing strategies from my writing where I only saw the words of a good story. I wrote Esther's song, "You Memorize Me," because you critiqued my work and heard music. I can't wait to celebrate with you when you finish your own book, *Tucker Hollow Road.*

Amber Lanier Nagle, you are a shining jewel amidst the gems in in our group. An engineer turned author and editor with a heart to encourage other writers. You've taken some of my clumsy attempts to write and with simple ease turned them into beauty. I love the times you've taught the group. Your style makes concepts understandable and accessible. I rewrote the beginning of so many chapters after your workshop on the use of hooks. Your fingerprint is probably on most of the books coming out of our talented writers' group. Your willingness to help get *Grief is Not My Future* to press is appreciated beyond words.

Ge-Anne Bolhuis, my Google Guru, thank you for sharing yourself so generously with not only our group, but with me as I neared the finish line the end of March. You helped me set up my FB Author page to share Esther's story with people during a frightening time around the world as COVID19 set in. You are a treasure.

Deck Cheatham and Kay Whatley, you two have been a more recent joy to me as cheer leaders and newer critique partners. Thanks for all your contributions to the group as well as to me personally. Your interest in Esther's story and positive input has blessed me many times over.

Terrisa Coleman, your gift of spiritual insights along with your love of story and reading, gave me some great critiques on a large portion of this book. Thank you for your generous gift, when as a pastor's wife and pastor in your own right had days already overflowing with responsibilities.

Margaret Sims, my beautiful friend, scholar, and teacher with the loveliest British accent I've ever heard. I learned so much in the times I met with you. How I would love to have taken a class in creative writing under you. Yet, your kind instruction and encouragement still ring in my ears. (At the moment I feel I should check out how many times I've use the word "was"...and where do I place a semicolon again?)

Pam Black, a long-time, dear friend of at least forty years, you've blessed me with your present presence as I so needed a prayer warrior, beta reader, and encourager. You came weekly after writing out your comments, read my story back to me so I could hear it in someone else's voice. What an experience, as I realized the depth of what God had done. The tear-soaked trail and strenuous climb of the last years had an anointing and depth, with words and phrases, beyond my ability. How good to know God's encouraging presence in those moments. Thank you for your time, talent and many prayers.

Karen Freeman, you've been a faithful friend for so long, I can barely remember you not being in my life. Thank you for your encouragement and your ear when all I could do was spill my wrenching emotions and pain. You quietly listened and didn't try to fix me. You gave me the space and grace time and again to be real. You've picked up the tab for meals time and again plus brought your wonderful homemade soups and dishes to my doorstep. Your loving support has meant the world to me

Dr. Melissa Hubbard, my dear faithful friend. How many years of friendship and words of wisdom have you generously given? You've walked me through so many of my critical life crisis' when life turned sideways and took me down unexpected tangled paths. You walked out the most devastating moments of my life as you offered your help, prayers, wit and wisdom 24/7 during Esther's illness, last days, and beyond. Thank you, seems way too inadequate. Forever grateful for you dear friend.

Pam Lord, my dear long-time friend of incredible intellect, Godly wisdom, and mastery of the English language. Your overall brilliance has always been inspiring and intimidating. You are just **so** smart. I've always stood in awe of your teaching skills in the great world of academia—so your praise and encouragement as you read my book has been an extraordinary boost to this newbie author. Thank you for lending me your expertise as you did a final in-depth correction of all the minutiae of my manuscript. Forever thankful!

Faye Martin, you've been a more recent friend, but one who knows the agony of losing a daughter. Your pain and circumstances were different, but you know the deep sorrow and the struggle of learning to breathe again. God brought you into my life at just the right time to add the spice and realism as you challenged me to say it better. What a treasure you have been to me as I neared the finish line. Your knowledge and skill of the written word has been the cherry on the top of my efforts. You've been my cheerleader and greatest fan as I neared the finish line. You have fallen in love with Esther as I have with your Lisa. Won't we have a grand time celebrating together when we are reunited with them in heaven?

Katrina (Lanette), my dear sister who I love and appreciate more than words on a page can convey. I tear up as I think of all the multiple ways you've come along side and supported me through the years. Chick trips to the ocean, thoughtful gifts so perfect for the moment, your presence during good times and hard times. Your caring heart, phone calls, prayers, and love for all three of our girls. Your special connection with Esther through the love of family history, music, and nature, blesses me so much. You've brought such a richness to my life since the moment you were born. Thank you for always showing up.

To My Oklahoma Cowboy, husband, lover, and dearest friend. This book may have been written without you at first—the pain, heartbreak, loss, and thrashing you suffered were so beyond imagination. But little by little you were drawn in as you began to heal. I know this book would have never seen the light of day without your support, wise insights, and spiritual knowledge, especially for the reflection and application sections at the end of each story. God knew what He was doing when He put us together. We make an amazing team.

Thank you for giving me the freedom and space to take all the time I needed to process my grief and learn this new skill of writing well. I know we could have used the extra income to replenish as our retirement years were upon us. But you encouraged me even though the bi-monthly trips, and often more, to North Georgia didn't make sense at the time. You are my best cheerleader and encourager—so patient with all my meltdowns and crazy moods. I love you best and forever.

About the Author

RayneJaynePhotography

Is it ever too late to begin again? To travel and experience cultures and sights you've only heard about? Go back to school for a degree? Begin a new vocation late in life? "Never!" Says Marla.

As a shy and quiet child, Marla watched the chatterboxes of her world with awe. Words flowed like an unending supply of water over Niagara Falls. She wondered, *where do their words come from? How do they know what to say and when? Do they rehearse?* Simply put, words scared her. What if she said the wrong thing? What if she sounded stupid or hurt someone's feelings?

Many years later, sitting among published and aspiring authors, no one could have been more surprised than she. Unlike many scribes who knew from an early age they were *supposed* to write, she had no such inclination. .

Then events entered her life and became a burgeoning landscape of words she knew must be put on paper to inspire and encourage others in their times of grief. Her inspiration to forge ahead with this book was born by experiencing God's tender presence amidst intense anguish. An experience which taught her intimacy with God in suffering is more valuable than enjoying temporary material blessings.

Marla spent most of her life in music education and ministry while raising a complex trio of daughters. Grief is Not My Future is based on the experiences surrounding her youngest, Esther.

Most of her life, the beautiful state of Georgia has been her home. She enjoys townhome-living atop a small mountain with a view that inspires her daily. Her husband is a constant source of gracious patience and support. *Grief is Not My Future* would never have seen the light of day without his insights, wit, and encouragement.

Marla has been a member of CAW, Calhoun Area Writers, GWA, Georgia Writers Association, and CAG, the Christian Authors Guild, with several stories published in Calhoun's yearly anthologies, "Telling Stories 1, 2, and 3." (available on Amazon)

One of Marla's greatest joys, is to hear from you. She welcomes your questions, comments, and loves to support others in their life's journey.
(By the way…tears don't scare her.)

Contact: marla@griefisnotmyfuture.com